THE
GOLDEN
RULES
OF HUMAN RESOURCE
MANAGEMENT

THE
GOLDEN
RULES
OF HUMAN RESOURCE
MANAGEMENT

**WHAT EVERY MANAGER
OUGHT TO KNOW . . .**

ALI ASADI, MBA, MA (IT)

authorHOUSE®

AuthorHouse™
1663 Liberty Drive
Bloomington, IN 47403
www.authorhouse.com
Phone: 1-800-839-8640

Published by AuthorHouse   04/14/2012

ISBN: 978-1-4685-8524-7 (sc)
ISBN: 978-1-4685-8525-4 (e)

Library of Congress Control Number: 2012906889

Table of Contents

This book is dedicated to my loving parents, Mohammad & Ashraf. Without their knowledge, wisdom, and guidance, I would not have the goals I have to strive for and the determination to be the best that I can be to reach my dreams!

Acknowledgments

Any book, even a small one such as this, cannot be produced without help and guidance from a number of people. In writing this book, I, too, have received much guidance and help, which I gratefully acknowledge. Here are some people I wish to thank by name.

My parents, Mohammad and Ashraf, who taught me that a business's most important asset is its people.

I wish to thank my teachers who have been such a great inspiration and who taught me to think clearly and logically and prepared me to chart my own path. In particular, I want to name Dr. Brain Dely and Louise Stelma.

I also want to thank Sanjay Srivastava for his contribution and Doug Russell for doing a great job in editing this book.

Thank you all. I look forward to your continued support.

Preface

Why another book on HR management?

As I went through my day-to-day work, I often found myself wanting practical guidance in HR management. All the thousands of books written by management gurus contained the information I sought, but it was seldom organized in a form where one could refer to the information without going through lengthy theory, case studies, surveys, and graphs.

Since I was lacking such an easy-to-use resource for HR information, I decided to get working and produce such a book myself. After all, if I felt this need, surely there were other busy managers out there who have no time to read lengthy management books in the hope of finding what they're looking for.

This book is a toolkit. If you seek an answer to your HR needs, you will find it here. If you need a specific form or a policy, you will find a template here, and if you want advice or a smart quote, you will find it here too.

Browse through the book as you will, use the table of contents, flip the pages, or just open on a random page. I am sure you will find something useful, something you did not know earlier.

Ali Asadi, MBA, MA (IT)

I wish you a happy journey of discovery and look forward to feedback and suggestions for additional sections.

Ali Asadi
Asadi Business Consulting
www.aprofitmaker.com

About the Author

 Ali Asadi is a well-known and respected author and professional business consultant. As the owner of Asadi Business Consulting, a management consultancy firm, he specializes in helping small and medium-size businesses achieve success in today's highly competitive business environment. He has more than fifteen years of business management experience and focuses on all aspects of business management consulting, and coaching. Ali is particularly knowledgeable and exceptionally skillful in analyzing your particular business needs and developing innovative techniques and proactive processes that can add value to your organization and increase profit potential.

He takes a personal, hands-on approach, working directly with owners and senior executives to fine-tune business strategies for maximum benefit to you and your business.

Ali holds a B.S. degree in civil engineering and master's degrees in business administration and information technology. He currently lives in Los Angeles, California, and is frequently active in community affairs and enjoys helping business owners and others across a wide range of private, public, and nonprofit organizations. Ali Asadi is truly a man of the people.

Visit his website at www.aprofitmaker.com. As you read this book, you may have specific questions about how to apply the tips, tools, ideas, and strategies that the author discusses. Please email your questions to Ali Asadi at ali@aprofitmaker.com. He will respond promptly and directly to you.

Section 1

Hiring

1.   Why Is Hiring So Important?

Hiring employees is easy! Correcting mistakes is what takes time. Any business that is not solely managed by family will need to hire employees. The decision will impact your business—one way or the other.

If you are a large business, one hiring error may not matter too much, unless it is the CEO! However, for entrepreneurs and SMEs, each worker represents a major fraction of the workforce. In a small organization, each employee represents a major fraction of the human resource. This means that while hiring correctly is important for all organizations, it becomes critical for small ones.

> *We built the Starbucks brand first with our people, not with consumers. Because we believed the best way to meet and exceed the expectations of our customers was to hire and train great people. We invested in employees.*
>
> **Howard Schultz, Starbucks Chairman**

Most business leaders—at least the ones who are progressive— recognize that it's employees who make the company. No matter how good you are, unless you are running a mom-and-pop store, your employees will face customers.

1

Employees will generate invoices. Employees will handle complaints, and employees will produce goods.

Entrepreneurs who ignore employees and the critical importance of getting the right employees will soon be without both the employees and their business!

> *If I were running a company today, I would have one priority above all others: to acquire as many of the best people as I could.*
>
> **Jim Collins, in *Good to Great***

Take your time to hire. It is better to go with a vacant chair for a few days than it is to fill it with the wrong person.

Hiring a new employee takes preparation. Other employees also watch. Therefore, it is extremely important that you have an established system in place for bringing in a new worker.

The Golden Rules

- No business survives without employees.
- The wrong employee costs you time, money, *and future business.*
- Do not initiate the hiring process without preparation.
- Get as many great employees as you can hire.
- Even if you are running a small store, put a hiring process into place.
- A wrong hire is disruptive to your business. It could cost 3 to 15 times the worker's salary to get a replacement. Choose with care.
- Employees meet more of your customers than you do. Your customers' impression of your business depends on your employees.
- A bad employee can affect many others. Hire with care.
- Your best practices will remain theories unless great employees put them into practice.
- By having a well-defined hiring process, you will find it easier to track the progress of recruitment throughout its various stages.

- Nothing you do will be more important than getting the right people into the right jobs.
- The more carefully you plan the hiring process, the fewer problems you will encounter during and after the hiring.

Remember, wrong employee selection will:

- × Make you lose customers
- × Add stress to the environment
- × Waste your training and mentoring
- × Miss opportunities
- × Possibly add to your legal and financial burdens

> *To decide where to drive the bus before you have the right people on the bus, and the wrong people off the bus, is absolutely the wrong approach.*
>
> **Jim Collins, in** *Good To Great*

2. Timing Your Hiring Actions

On some occasions, it is very clear that you need to hire a new worker. The vacancy exists due to promotion or maybe someone has left or has been fired. On all of these occasions, you should be in a position to anticipate the vacancy and take actions to start the hiring process in time.

A process that starts under control will go better. If you can anticipate and plan your hiring actions, you will generally get a better candidate than if you run out in the street when the chair falls vacant. Remember—and we will emphasize this time and again—a planned and controlled process will get you better results every time.

If you are creating a new position, timing can be more difficult. Slowly, over the course of day-to-day business, you realize that you are understaffed in a specific area. Do remember that employees have to generate much more than their salary in output just to cover the wages you give them. Be sure you have the work available for them to contribute enough.

Do the math. Apart from the salary and bonuses and any other perks, do you have the space, furniture, and workstation that will be essential for your new employee? Consider the training required to bring the employee up to speed. If the training program is run on predetermined dates, it makes no sense to make new hires report much ahead of that date unless you can put them to work before the training session.

Many times seasonal issues also dominate your hiring decisions. Stores take on extra help before the holiday season starts, and so do many businesses. Financial consultants need more accountants just before the close of the year. These needs can be planned for—and therefore done better. Select your hires well before the season starts, and you will get the best ones.

The Golden Rules

- Make sure you start the hiring process in time.
- Ensure you have the resources—more so if you are creating a new job. There are many hidden and visible expenses before an employee becomes productive.
- Be aware of your seasonal needs.
- Dovetail your new employee's arrival with the start of scheduled training programs.

3. Determine Your Needs

Determine what jobs you need done and what skills are needed.

The first step in the hiring process is to determine your needs. Write out the qualifications (duties/responsibilities, skills/expertise needed, experience and education/training required or desired) for the position you are trying to fill. Pay some attention to the type of personality of the individual you are looking to hire. For example, you need a different personality for a researcher as compared with a salesperson. Prioritize the needs and the qualifications you seek, and this will help you create a good job description.

Identify the responsibilities in each area where the need exists and the skill that is required to fulfill this gap. Look at education, knowledge, and skills, (such as bookkeeping, computer usage capability—what hardware/software?), communicating (writing, speaking, making presentations), leading/supervising.

For each area of responsibility, determine the personal characteristics required for each job (such as attention to detail, organized, personable, persuasive, insightful, able to work independently).

You should consider the result that you expect from that job and then go backward to find out the qualifications needed for it. Sometimes, you need to have two people for the job.

Consider that the job must be doable. Do not be a perfectionist and expect too much from a single person. If you find the work description is getting too complex, consider creating two jobs.

Keep in mind that knowledge and the ability to do the job are not the same things.

The Golden Rules

- Tabulate and prioritize your requirements.
- Identify responsibilities and the skills required.
- If needed, break up complex jobs into two.

4.   Sample Job Rating Form

Once you have defined the requirements of the job, prioritize your hiring criteria and make a rating form based on the requirements you have tabulated. The values will form a typical 5-point Likert Scale, with

1 representing "weak" and 5 representing "strong." You can give ratings the following objective values:

  1—Low requirement, an unimportant criterion
  2—Below-average requirement, not critical
  3—Acceptable, required criterion
  4—Above-average, important requirement
  5—Essential requirement

How can you ever place any requirement in the low-requirement category? Here's an example: if you are recruiting security guards, physical attributes are important, but educational requirements are relatively unimportant. However, if you are recruiting knowledge workers, then the opposite will apply.

Sample Criteria-Marking Chart

Job Title	Availability	Education & Skills	Experience	Employment History	Salary Sought	Total

The Golden Rules

- Defining the requirements of the job well will allow you to frame a comprehensive job-rating form.
- Since the requirements are different for different jobs, the job-rating form will change as well.

5. Defining the Job

This is another step that helps you think more about your needs and the job you are seeking to fill. Once a need for a new employee has been established, you start the process of the actual hiring. If you are a large, well-established organization, your task is in some ways easier, while in others it may well be more complex.

It is easier in large organizations because there are well-defined qualifications, duties, responsibilities, and salary bands in place. It may be more difficult because the procedures may be lengthier. Autonomy to one HR manager may be subject to validations and approvals.

As mentioned earlier, your staffing decision can be more critical to your company if you are small. Therefore, preparation and careful selection are important. However, remember that a small firm needs greater flexibility than a larger organization. Be sure that you leave flexibility in your job definition.

Create a detailed job description—If the position has become vacant due to a promotion, you should ask the person promoted to write a detailed job description for you. Sometimes, you will be surprised at the level of detail you will get—something an HR manager may never otherwise know. People who are being promoted will naturally do their best for your company. In fact, every time you promote employees, you should ask them to detail their previous job requirements explicitly.

> *The only job where you start at the top is digging a hole.*
>
> **Source Unknown**

Do not restrict yourself to the previous employee alone; ask the boss to give you a job description as well.

In the case where you are creating a new job, you have more work writing a good job description. Write what you can decide on, discuss it with other managers in similar businesses, and discuss it with the person the new hire will be working with. Another good place to look for job specifications can be the classified ads for similar positions placed by other companies in the same business.

Once your job description is clear, work out the salary package and the other tangible/intangible benefits you will be offering the individual. A number of websites allow you to research salary packages. If your employees can research salaries, so can you! Knowing what others pay could be helpful too.

<u>Appendix A</u> gives you a sample job description and the work you need to do before placing an ad. Take a look.

The Golden Rules

- A well-defined job will get you better-qualified candidates.
- Ensure you leave scope for additional duties in the job description.
- Ask the previous incumbent (where possible) to give you a job description. Ask the boss as well.
- Check out what the industry does as well.
- Research the salary and fix the salary band and benefits you will offer.

6. Writing Job Ads

A well-written job ad has other advantages besides attracting the applicants you want. By being specific, it gets you responses from those who meet your basic criteria—thereby saving you time reading piles of CVs or interviewing candidates who do not meet your requirements. A good ad also works as a banner for your company even though some people who read it may not be interested in applying.

We know that good employees are critical to a company. Therefore, the success of a job ad can be best ascertained by the quality of the candidates it is likely to bring in. For example, if you are looking for top-quality researchers, your ad will emphasize the field of research, facilities, intellectual freedom, previous patents, and support staff. If this is done well and the ad is displayed in the right media, you can be sure to get good responses.

The media you use—print or online—will depend on the job you are offering. For most jobs, the norm now is to use both media. This way you reach both the Internet users and people who do not use the Internet. An online ad can be more detailed and have links to a greater amount of information, whereas a print ad is often smaller and more

---

direct due to the higher costs involved. For print ads, be sure to give offline methods of applying (fax and surface mail) besides giving an email address and a website.

Even when you are writing for the Internet, do not make your ad overly detailed and long. It will turn off many prospects. Use bulleted text, white space, and indenting to make your text easier to read. Give a great title that attracts attention (both print and online).

You can combine several vacancies in one ad, but be sure that they are targeting similar groups. If you need administrative and accounting staff they can fit together, this ad cannot contain a posting for a CFO or an IT head because they may not be looking at the media where your ad is published.

The Golden Rules

- Write a conversational advertisement—do not make the advertisement too complex or stiff.
- Use the direct pronoun "you." You are selling your company to the would-be hire. Employ sales language to attract the best

possible talent. This is particularly important if you are looking for special and hard-to-find talent. As an example, we could say "On this job, you will have complete freedom to research and publish." Contrast this with "Candidate will be allowed to research and publish."

- Keep the ad precise, without any fluff—stay to the point and crisp.
- Double-check for errors.
- Avoid giving a sales pitch; do not make inflated claims about a great work environment and benefits.
- Describe benefits and career-advancement opportunities.
- Offer multiple contact methods.
- Combine vacancies but sensibly; you cannot expect facility management people and database administrators to scan the same advertisement spaces.

7.   Posting a Job

A key decision to be made early in the hiring process is whether you are going to post a job to the external world or first declare the vacancy internally.

There are pros and cons to each option, and in some cases one or the other approach may be nearly mandatory. There are cases where the morale of your existing employees makes it necessary that you give them an opportunity to be promoted first. Only when a suitable internal candidate is not found should you go for an external hire. Following this policy allows you to retain experience not to mention avoiding trouble with unions.

Especially in a large organization, it makes more sense to promote an employee than to hire a newcomer. You know the person; the employee knows the company and its culture and in all probability knows part of the job anyway. Getting the employee to be productive in the new position will be far faster than starting someone from ground zero.

There will be cases where it is absolutely necessary to bring in fresh blood. Your organization may be small with insufficient numbers of employees to really promote anyone. The job description may be something totally new, or you may want to break away from the traditional way of doing things. Steve Jobs did that when he brought in John Sculley from Pepsi to run Apple.

> *Are you going to sell sugar water for the rest of your life or come with me and change the world?*
>
> **Steve Jobs to John Sculley, as recounted in Sculley's book, *Odyssey: Pepsi to Apple***

If you decide on an internal selection first, the office email and bulletin board are obvious choices to let employees know. Word of mouth also works in small organizations. However, make the requirements of the job and the qualifications and experience required very clear. Give adequate time for people to update their resumes and apply.

If you decide to look outside for your new employee, your methods will depend on the job you are advertising.

Since you are looking for the best-possible person to fill a vacancy, pay some attention to the way you publicize it. For someone to fill a technology position, online job portals and social networking sites will provide good results. For really senior-level positions, a headhunter or a consultant may give far better results. Quite often, your own employees may refer a good prospect.

As mentioned elsewhere in this book, make it easy for applicants to contact you. Whenever possible, accept applications online only since it allows for faster screening and processing. If you are offering a fax option, ensure the fax is loaded with paper (especially when you are locking up and over weekends) and is kept in a location that is not public.

You can locate prospects using your business contacts and networks. Your own hiring manager may have resumes kept from previous job postings or may be able to obtain these from other companies. Your managers may be able to provide referrals as well.

Consider developing an employee referral program. You can reward employees for identifying prospective employees for hard-to-fill positions. Just as you would do in an internal hiring program, make your requirements very clear before the start of the referral process.

Other options include putting up "Help Wanted" signs if you have a high-traffic workplace. Getting graduating students from colleges is another good idea. You will need to develop a relationship with the career center director or internship coordinator to ensure that you are welcomed to the college. Do not assume that just because you are looking for only a few candidates, you will not be considered. Colleges are concerned about placements, and if you offer a challenging job with learning and growth prospects, they will be glad to help you.

The Golden Rules

- There are pros and cons to both internal and external hiring.
- Ask your employees to publicize the position through their online social media networks.
- Place a classified advertisement in appropriate newspapers.
- Post the position on job—and newspaper-related websites—include the company website.
- Post the position on professional association websites.
- Contact university career centers.
- Use recruitment agencies when justified.

8.   Creating Structured Application Forms

Did you notice the "application forms" in an earlier section?

Let's say you have a great opening, you put up a great ad, and you get a great many responses. Everyone writes essays and submits a CV. You are now left with the unenviable task of comparing apples, oranges, and potatoes. This can be avoided if you create a structured application. Working under pressure may cause you to miss out on someone important if you neglect to do this.

A structured application form allows you to obtain data in the same format from every candidate. If you can do this online, then it is even better, since all data can go into a database from where comparison and evaluation is simple. Even if your applications are on paper, comparison and evaluation of candidates is far easier. Your application form should be based on your needs (from the rating form) and the job description you have written.

If you want to see an example, look at the admission forms of any Ivy League college. They get applications in the tens of thousands from every corner of the world. The applicants are people with diverse educational standards, cultures, and levels of English. If there were no standardization, the admission process would never get completed.

The structure of application forms will vary and depend on the position you are offering. Most often, the application form will have two parts—the first relates to general data about the candidate and can be in a standard format. The second part is specific to the job you are offering.

You can often ask the department that is initiating the hiring to create the second part. This ensures that the right questions are asked of the candidate. A typical application form (first part) can be seen in <u>Appendix B</u> of this book.

Since the second part of the application is specific to the particular job, it can often be customized by the department looking for the new employee. Since they know the job best, they should write the specs. You should standardize this form to give it the same look and feel as the first part and remove any redundancies between them.

The Golden Rules

- Ensure that your application form makes it easy to assess and compare candidates.
- If possible, accept forms online with data going directly into a database. This ensures easy compilation and comparison and makes record maintenance easier.
- Ensure that you have an offline method to accept forms too—typically fax and snail mail.
- The domain specialist must create part 2 of the form to capture relevant education.

9.   Shortlisting Candidates

Doing this is not too difficult if your applications are standardized and designed well. This process will end when you have a list of candidates qualified enough to be called for interviews.

The shortlisting process consists of two parts—in the first, you select all candidates who meet your general criteria. This is the bar all candidates must cross to be considered. Here you simply ensure that the candidate has the educational and skill levels,

> *Which one of the three candidates would you want your daughter to marry?*
>
> **H. Ross Perot**

meets the citizenship requirements, and so on. You are not checking to determine how good employees are at doing their work or if they can do the required work. That is a task for the technical vetting team.

The first stage of shortlisting reduces the long pile of applications to a smaller stack. The shortened list is now examined by the domain expert to select applicants qualified enough to be called in for an interview.

Rating Applications

If you have structured your application well, rating your candidates is easier.

You can then make a rating form based on the requirements you have listed in the advertisement. The values will form a typical 5-point Likert Scale, with 1 representing "weak" and 5 representing "strong." You can give ratings the following objective values:

> 1—Low capability
> 2—Below-average capability
> 3—Acceptable capability
> 4—Above-average capability
> 5—Exceptional capability

For each of the criterion you have specified, rank each candidate on this scale. (This is assuming you give equal weight to each capability. If some attribute is twice as important as another, multiply by two to give you the correct ranking.)

Add the marks for each candidate, and sort the list in descending order (highest marks first) to create a merit list. You can now decide how many candidates from the list you want to call for the interview or further follow-up.

Sample Applicants Rating Form

Applicant	Availability	Education & Skills	Experience	Employment History	Requested Salary	Total
A						
B						
C						

The Golden Rules

- A good application management system makes it easy to assess a large number of applications.
- Once the applications have been rated and ranked, it becomes easy for technical experts/domain specialists to decide who to call for an interview. A fair selection is ensured because marks are given objectively.
- There are mandatory qualities (such as honesty, good attitude, positive thinking) that are essential. Do not waste time with applicants who do not have these.

10. Interviewing Candidates

This is one of the most important jobs you are called on to do in HR. Here is what you must (and must not) do.[1]

Let's assume you have a well-defined job vacancy to fill, and from the large numbers of resumes that have come in, a selection of likely candidates has been made.

Most often, candidates are graded, and the most promising one is called in first. You could easily do it the other way around. Both approaches are beneficial.

> *So many people out there have no idea what they want to do for a living, but they think that by going on job interviews they'll magically figure it out. If you're not sure, that message comes out loud and clear in the interview.*
>
> **Todd Bermont,**
> **Renowned Job-Hunting Expert**

As a planning tool, allocate about 20 minutes for each interview. As part of the preparation for the interview, have a list of questions you will be asking every candidate and separate lists of questions for candidates

---

[1] How to Conduct a Job Interview, New York State Department of Civil Service, available at *http://www.cs.state.ny.us*.

to clarify points from the applications or to test their understanding of particular issues.

The questions should be typed. Keep paper and pens ready for the candidates in case they need them. Copies of the CV, a job description, and the company brochure should also be on hand.

Arrange the interview room well. It reflects on your company culture. Set your candidate at ease by providing a quiet place without any distractions and uncomfortable seating. Just as you would not expect the interviewee to be taking calls during the interview, your secretary should also not be connecting any calls to *you* during the interview.

It is important to break the ice and set a friendly tone for the interview. Introduce yourself and any other members of the interviewing team, and explain your function in the organization. Spend two minutes or so in building rapport and talking about some things you may have in common. This could be experience in the same field, a common interest, industry news, or something similar. The idea is to start a conversation and let the applicant talk.

Control over the interview is with you all along. You make the transition from small talk to hard topics. It is easiest to introduce the opportunity the job offers and say where the candidate fits or not.

You can ask questions for about 10 to 15 minutes. If you are well prepared, the questions will be relevant to the resume, fill in gaps, and let you explore the candidate's skills and experience. You can state where you feel the candidate is lacking in required strengths, and let the candidate respond to that.

Making the candidate speak is important. After all, you want to hear this person talk about their skills and the work they are going to do. Ask open-ended questions rather than ones that can be answered with a simple "yes" or "no."

Most often, the following questions will have to be asked:

- What are your career goals?
- What are you really good at professionally?
- What are you not good at or not interested in doing professionally?
- Who were your last five bosses, and how will they each rate your performance on a 1 to 10 scale when we talk to them?
- What was the position you held?
- Who were the people you worked with?
- Tell us about yourself (background, education, work history, skills)
- What were your duties at your last job?
- What did you like about your last job?
- What did you not like about your last job?
- Why did you leave your last job?
- What accomplishments are you most proud of?
- What are your strengths?
- What are your weaknesses?
- Why should we hire you?
- What do you know about our company?
- Do you prefer to work alone or with other people?
- Where do you see yourself in the next three years?
- How do you describe yourself?

Equally important, there are certain questions that you *cannot* ask. Equal Employment Opportunity Commission (EEOC) guidelines, as well as federal and state laws, prohibit asking certain questions of a job applicant, either on the application form or during the interview. These are questions such as:

- × Age or date of birth (if interviewing a teenager, you can ask if he or she is 16 years old)
- × Sex, sexual orientation, race, creed, color, religion, or national origin
- × Credit history
- × Disabilities of any kind
- × Date and type of military discharge
- × Marital status
- × Maiden name (for female applicants)

× If a person is a citizen (you *can* ask, however, if he or she has the legal right to work in the United States)

× How many children do you have? How old are they? Who will care for them while you are at work?

× Have you ever been treated by a psychologist or psychiatrist?

× Have you ever been treated for drug addiction or alcoholism?

× Have you ever been arrested? (You may, however, ask if the person has been convicted of a crime so long as you accompany the question with the statement that a conviction will not necessarily disqualify an applicant for employment.)

× How many days were you sick last year?

× Have you ever filed for workers' compensation? Have you ever been injured on the job?

It is better to err on the side of caution if in doubt about the correctness of a question. On some occasions, these questions can be asked. For example, if you are interviewing someone for a financial opening, credit history can be relevant. An arrest history can be relevant if the job involves working with children and so on. Seek legal advice if in doubt.

Make notes during the interview. Do this for all candidates so that at the end of each interview you can prepare a tabulated listing of marks[2] and use it later to decide an order of merit. Even if you have found an ideal candidate, continue to record your marking for every other candidate. It has often happened that the star candidate declines to join, and then you are left racking your memory! A sample evaluation sheet is available at Appendix C.

Red Flags and Warning Signs:

Many warning signs should not be ignored unless the candidate has a very good explanation or a reason:

---

[2] How to Conduct a Job Interview, New York State Department of Civil Service, available at *http://www.cs.state.ny.us.*

× Arriving late for the interview
× Treating your staff disrespectfully
× Talking too much
× Not wearing appropriate clothing
× Speaking negatively about past employers
× Asking about money too soon
× Showing up unprepared
× Using inappropriate language
× Being unclear in responses
× Not asking any questions

Depending on the complexity of the job being offered, you could hold several rounds of interviews. Some could be to check technical or domain knowledge, others could be to negotiate terms and assess suitability of the "fit." For senior appointments, there will invariably be a number of rounds before an offer is made.

11. Conducting Tests

Before you conduct any tests as part of an interview process, follow the rules listed below.

If tests are required to be administered, make sure they are standard tests that are relevant to the job description and are applied to all candidates. If you are using a vendor to do this, check their credentials carefully. Read through the test to ensure that there are no racial/gender/nationality or other biases. You could take advice from others who have done this as well.

Be aware that there are limits on testing, and laws govern some testing. Seek legal advice where necessary.

The Golden Rules

• Mention the test in the letter calling the candidate for the interview so that candidates are adequately prepared.

- Ensure that the same test is administered to all the candidates (at a later stage no one should be able to raise an issue of discrimination).
- Hold the test for all the applicants together using a common question paper.

12. Reference Checks

In the application form, you would have already received consent from the applicant to proceed with job verification and reference checks. The candidate would have also given you the names of two or more references and explicitly given you permission to contact his or her previous employer.

Check with the most recent employer first. Many employers only give out details of employment and dates of hiring and leaving. When you get a person of appropriate seniority on the line, tell them who you are and the reason for your call. Ask if you can discuss the candidate and assure confidentiality. Inform the person about the position for which the applicant is being considered so that he or she can give a more accurate evaluation of the applicant.

After you have given background information about the position you are looking to fill, ask some general-response questions, such as "How do you think the applicant would fit into our position?" Once the person responds, ask more specific questions.

Let the person talk freely as long as he or she wants without interruption.

Watch for obvious pauses in answers. This is often a sign that further questions on the same subject may get more detailed answers.

Record the responses in a standardized form; a format is available at
Appendix D.[3]

Questions that can be asked if the previous employer is forthcoming
with information:

- How long have you known the candidate? In what relationship/
  capacity?
- What was the candidate's position? To whom did he or she
  report?
- What were the candidate's responsibilities? Scope?
- How did the candidate get along with superiors, peers, and
  subordinates?
- Describe the candidate's attitudes and other personality
  factors.
- What were some of the candidate's outstanding
  accomplishments?
- How effective was the candidate in terms of quantity and quality
  of work?
- How creative was the candidate? How much initiative did he or
  she display?
- Motivation level? Resourcefulness?
- Describe the candidate's leadership ability and responsibility
  levels.
- What were the candidate's strengths? Aptitudes? Weaknesses?
- How well does the candidate express himself or herself orally?
  In writing?
- Did the candidate meet deadlines?
- What was the candidate's salary? Did he or she receive any
  bonuses?
- Why did the candidate leave?
- Would you be willing to rehire him or her?

In many cases, you can find out a lot about your prospect from social
networking sites such as Facebook. Professional networking sites, such

---

[3] How to Conduct a Job Interview, New York State Department of Civil
Service, available at *http://www.cs.state.ny.us.*

22

as LinkedIn, also provide considerable information. From these sites, you can learn much about the affiliations, attitude, and knowledge level of the candidate. If you are interviewing a candidate for a technical position and find the person is maintaining an authoritative blog, and that the blog is citied by a number of other experts, you can be reasonably sure of the technical credentials of the candidate.

The Golden Rules

- Inform the candidate during the initial phase of application that you need references and will be speaking with them.
- Ask for work references. Do not waste your time asking for personal references. No one will give you names of people who will have something negative to say.
- Require consent in writing. Make it a part of your application form. Ensure that the form is structured in such a way that it is only complete when the references section is completed.
- Do not consider the application further if the candidate refuses to supply references.

13. Making a Decision

For almost every job, there is competition between employers to get the right candidates. Therefore, you need to make your decision quickly and complete the hiring process rapidly and consistent with the qualifications you are looking for.

Be quick about putting together all the marking sheets, evaluations, references, and resumes and arriving at a final answer. Companies that have a long-drawn-out approval process may lose out on good candidates unless the reputation of the company is such that a candidate is willing to wait for you.

The Golden Rules

- Good documentation maintained throughout the hiring process will help you in making a good decision.
- It is important to be crisp in decision-making.
- The selection process itself tells your new recruit a great deal about your company's work culture.

14. Making a Job Offer

Having completed all the required interviews, tests, and background checks, you are finally ready to make an offer to the selected candidate. Since good employees can have several other options, it is important that an offer be made quickly. If you are sure about the person you have selected, make an offer and close the selection process. For individuals paid by the hour, a spot offer can be made. You can also do this for salaried positions although normally for such positions one expects a negotiation and formal settlement of terms and benefits.

Make any terms and conditions very clear. Companies normally start negotiation with about 80 to 90 percent of the maximum they expect to pay. Most candidates, especially the ones in senior positions, will ask for a larger amount, and negotiation will follow to fix an amount that is acceptable to all.

Keep track of the final amount agreed upon, and record the information. There have been occasions where the final-offer letter mentions something at variance with what has been agreed to. Besides being embarrassing, it sends a totally wrong message to the new employee.

A sample job-offer letter is available at Appendix E

The Golden Rules

- The hiring process may appear lengthy, but it is a necessary investment.

- The cost of a wrong hire could be several times the annual salary.
- Obtain any required authorizations for salary and perks before salary negotiations start unless you have the authority to make spot offers.
- At the end of a protracted negotiating session, summarize the job offer for everyone to see.
- There have been occasions when the offer letter has different terms from what was agreed upon during the negotiation. Double-check.

Thank Other Applicants

Thank all applicants, especially those you interviewed. Provide a quick thank-you letter and thanks for their time, saying you are going to keep their information on file and that you'll let them know if any new positions become available.

A sample thank-you letter is available at Appendix F.

Section 2

Orientation and Onboarding

E very employee represents an investment.

How new employees are introduced to your environment will in many ways set the tone for how they will perform. There is no second chance to make a first impression. This applies to your company as well.

The new employee needs help and support to become acclimatized. If you want this process to take the least amount of time, it should be done fast and competently.

Even if the new employee has been selected from within your group, the person still needs orientation to settle into the new job.

Good employee orientation ensures:

- Understanding of what is important to your company
- Understanding of the company's core values
- Understanding of the employee's responsibilities
- Employee's ability to become productive faster
- Establishing a good working relationship

Taking control over the orientation and learning process is important because employees may learn the job from the wrong person! They might carry on previous work practices, which may be quite different from your company culture.

The first few days in a company can determine the success or failure of the employment relationship.

15. Orientation Essentials

Ideally, a manual should be given to every new employee. This manual should contain all information you'd like the employee to know, which can be reviewed at leisure and read whenever in doubt. It should contain:

- History, mission statement, and statement of values the company takes seriously
- Any policies and procedures the employee must know
- Safety rules
- Benefits and company perks that are common to all
- Work hours, leave and overtime rules, sick leave, etc.

Mail Room Orienter:

You punch in at 8:30 every morning, except you punch in at 7:30 following a business holiday, unless it's a Monday, then you punch in at 8:00 o'clock. Punch in late, and they dock you.

Incoming articles get a voucher; outgoing articles provide a voucher. Move any article without a voucher and they dock you. Letter size a green voucher, oversize a yellow voucher, parcel size a maroon voucher. Wrong color voucher and they dock you!

6787049A/6. That is your employee number. It will not be repeated! Without your employee number, you cannot get your paycheck.

Interoffice mail is code 37, intra-office mail 37-3, outside mail is 3-37. Code it wrong and they dock you!

This has been your orientation. Is there anything you do not understand? Is there anything you understand only partially? [spoken at about 160 words-per-minute]

Employee orientation scene from the movie, *The Hudsucker Proxy*

- Performance appraisal
- Dress code

Many organizations follow a buddy system, with new employees being given a buddy for the first few days. Selection of the buddy is done carefully. You want to show your best employee and not someone who is unhappy.

On the first day at work, every new employee should be greeted by an appropriate employee at your site. At the very minimum, do the following:

- A tour of the work area
- Introduction to coworkers at their place of work
- Briefing on keys, IDs, restrooms, entrances and exits, breaks
- Discussion with manager of job description, expectations, goals, regulations
- Details on security, using computer network, email. Instructions on use of Internet, mail, and removable media security. Registration of user account and creation of logins.
- Completion of all necessary insurance and payroll forms
- An informal coffee/ lunch if appropriate
- Going over the 5 C's of your business:
  - Customers (main customers, their demands and values)
  - Competitors (main competitors and their strengths)
  - Collaborators (suppliers and related businesses)
  - Company (company history, goals, and current situation)
  - The market climate (your industry)

A well-designed orientation program convinces new employees that the company is run efficiently, that they are cared for, and that the company is willing to invest time and money in them.

> *Most firms no longer operate under a "sink or swim" philosophy when it comes to employee learning. Instead, employees are oriented to the firm and later trained and developed.*
>
> **Andrew DuBrin**, in *Essentials of Management*

16. Training

No manager will ever contend that his subordinates will not benefit from available training. Even if you have well-trained personnel, giving them refresher training will help break bad habits and shortcuts acquired over time, and the discussion that training classes invariably generates will help spread best practices.

Even if you are moving employees from one office to another or promoting someone to take on additional responsibilities in the same domain, training needs cannot be overlooked.

Employees cannot be treated to a one-size-fits-all approach to training. Even new hires will need a degree of customized training based on their previous experience, skills, education, and talents. For all but the most trivial of tasks, employees want to know the right way to do a job and how it impacts the other work in your organization.

> *"Personally, I'm always ready to learn, although I do not always like being taught."*
>
> **Winston Churchill**

Merely giving them a lecture and showing some slides will not do. You must create a program that lets them practice the job under supervision, and if the task is really complex, provide follow-up training and perhaps videos they can view in their spare time.

A wise Chinese scholar once said, "Tell me, and I will remember for a while. Show me, and I will remember for longer. Let me do it, and I will never forget." Let that wisdom guide your training sessions.

It has also been observed that training employees makes them feel wanted in a company. The very fact that their company is investing in their development boosts morale and productivity. This directly translates into reduced turnover of employees.

The Golden Rules

- Training new employees well is extremely important since your new employees' productivity, safety, and organizational growth will depend on it. Do not delegate the task to a trainer who is inadequately trained, lacks morale, and is not keen on the task.
- If you do not have the right trainer, consider outsourcing the job.
- Create training notes, job videos, and manuals that employees can refer to. Insist on creating checklists for important and complex tasks.
- Test the employee and provide feedback during training sessions.
- Break up the training into phases. New employees may not be able to grasp it all at one time. Get them back for more advanced concepts once they have mastered the basics and been on the job for some time.
- Standardize the basic tasks.
- Give feedback at different stages of the training classes. This will allow you to take corrective action in time.
- Look for measurable improvement in employee performance. Know the parameters you should measure.

17. Setting up a Mentoring Program

> *I was sustained by one piece of inestimable good fortune.*
> *I had for a friend a man of immense and patient wisdom*
> *and a gentle but unyielding fortitude.*
>
> *I did not give in because he would not let me give in*
>
> **Thomas Wolfe**

Having a good mentoring program is an effective method of improving the training and culture of your organization. Mentoring has been in place for hundreds of years and has been one of the most effective ways of transferring tacit knowledge—that cannot be written down or codified to someone new to the job.

Mentoring is participative and inclusive. It builds relationships and imparts organizational values to your new employees.

Most people in your organization, even the star workers, are probably not good mentors. You must look for people who are able to establish relationships and rapport as well as command respect for their own quality of work.

When you are implementing a mentoring program, you will need to consider the following:

- Selection and training of mentors themselves. The requirement may not be much, but you will need to ensure that the mentors know their role. (Are they teaching how to assemble a widget or transferring a manufacturing culture or both?)
- How much time the mentor must spend away from the job.
- Managing the program, evaluating and monitoring progress, and benefits.

Section 3

Performance Management

Employee performance management is a process of leading and developing your employees to deliver the results that you want. It also involves motivating your employees and evaluating their performance so that the employee and the company are clear about present performance levels and what needs to be improved.

Good performance management is a process of partnership between employees and management. Both gain.

Typically, new employees will need about three months to become productive in their job. You need to ensure that they are well trained, comfortable, and can work independently. During this period, you will also be able to judge their caliber and the cultural fit between your company and the employee. Make it clear that you will be doing a performance review at 90 days to allow the employee to prepare. This date is not set in stone. You can vary it depending on the nature of the work. Some employees also settle in faster (or slower).

A key question is whether or not employees can relate their work to the company's mission and to customer satisfaction. If not, a shortfall has occurred in the initial orientation process. Take immediate corrective steps.

18. The Criticality of Performance Management

An effective performance management system is critical to ensure that the priorities of the employees and the company coincide. If variances are found, it is important to correct them as soon as possible and align the employee with company policy.

> *There are no shortcuts to any place worth going.*
>
> **Beverly Sills, American operatic soprano**

The customer is the key to all your operations. The company mission and employee satisfaction are important too—in that sequence. The performance management system aims to link employee actions to their internal/external customers and to the company's mission statement.

While evaluating your employees, you would be assessing their performance in a number of key fields. Some of these are shown below.

- Job knowledge
- Safety
- Quality of work
- Teamwork
- Communication
- Customer service
- Ability to meet goals
- Leadership
- Flexibility
- IT/equipment/machinery skills
- Time management

In most cases, you would define the relative importance of these attributes, depending on the nature of the job and the role of the employee. Other attributes could also be present.

19. Communication

> *Think like a wise man but communicate in the language of the people.*
>
> **WB Yeats, dramatist & poet (1865-1939)**

Sometimes, we forget that employees are not mind readers. Even the best-intentioned employees will only do what they think is the best for the company and its customers. Your job is to ensure that what the employee thinks is the best is really so.

Even when you are communicating extensively, make sure that the message reaching all employees is the message you are seeking to give. For example, you may do something to save money, while employees may take it to mean their jobs are not secure.

This kind of communication mismatch can occur for various reasons, including the following:

- Varying frames of reference
- Varying listening skills and distractions
- Personal variables, such as emotional state or prejudice
- Differences in message formats, making it difficult for all employees. Some may not be comfortable with email, for example, and may need to use printed copies

You will need to obtain regular and extensive feedback to ensure that all your employees are getting the same message. Failure to do so could lead to nasty surprises.

20. Ensure Receipt of Communication

Check back with your employees as to what they think you want them to do. This is called checking receipt of communication (ROC). You will be surprised at the variation you will sometimes hear even if you have just given out instructions. Use the opportunity to improve your messages so that ambiguity is eliminated.

> *Elegance of language may not be in the power of all of us; but simplicity and straight forwardness are. Write much as you would speak; speak as you think. If with your inferior, speak no coarser than usual; if with your superiors, no finer. Be what you say; and, within the rules of prudence, say what you are.*
>
> **Anonymous**

Spoken instructions are often interpreted differently because most employees will forget exactly what has been said and will work with the instructions as they remember them. For the really critical jobs, create a written instruction, which will ensure that even after several days, the employee can refer back to it, and this reduces the chances of making a mistake.

If your instructions are very clear, costly mistakes and rework will be minimized.

The Golden Rules

- Do not expect employees to be mind readers. Most employees want to excel. The difficulty is that they do not know clearly enough what they are required to do.
- Clear job descriptions and management expectations help to remove doubts.
- Goals must be SMART—specific, measurable, achievable, realistic, and timely.
- Do everything possible to get your team on the same page as you are.
- Setting performance expectations will be easier if you clarify the list below for your employees
  - What does a good job look like? Which results are satisfactory, and which are great?
  - You need to tell your employees why, what, and how to do the job.

- How is an employee expected to behave when performing a task?
- How long should it take to complete the job?
- Which are the likely safety issues?
- How can the job be performed in an economical manner?
- Does any company or other rules or regulations affect how the job should be performed?
- Make your performance expectations well known.
- Recognize top employees and value them and their work.
- If there is a performance and expectation mismatch, investigate before applying a quick fix.
- Employees must be able to make a direct connection between performance expectation and performance reviews. Ensure the performance review form is linked to the employee's job description.
- Discuss the performance review form with new employees on their first day at work. Occasionally discuss the form with your established employees to get feedback and improve the system further.

A sample performance review form is available at Appendix G.

21. Coaching Your Employees

Coaching your employees begins with providing effective feedback. Done well, it will boost employee performance and forms a major part of performance management activities.

> *I absolutely believe that people, unless coached, never reach their maximum capabilities.*
>
> **Bob Nardelli, CEO Home Depot**

You need to coach your employees regularly. Workers who get no feedback will either be disappointed that their efforts are not noticed or will assume that all is well.

Training is different from coaching in that training passes on skills and knowledge. When coaching, you provide feedback on performance and give pointers to improve performance.

The best coaches have a great sense of timing. Take the time to coach in the following situations:

- When an associate meets expectations
- When an employee exceeds expectations
- When there is a gap in performance
- Whenever you review performance

In short, you can coach on a continual basis.

22. Monitoring Performance

There are a number of ways to monitor performance. Naturally, you won't always follow any one of these but will adapt and change depending on the situation and employee. Here is a short list:

- Manage by walking around. Interact with your team, listen to them, talk to them, and take suggestions. As you develop rapport, you will have feedback and be able to assess your employees better.
- Review regularly. Since you will be looking at the problem from a wider perspective, you will be able to spot developing problems and anticipate areas of conflict. Consider this example: An oil company rented a drilling machine for $10,000 per day. One day the drill bit broke. Drill bits cost $100 apiece. Since the purchasing clerk did not know how critical the drill bit was for the job, he waited to order so that he could get ten drill bits for $90 per piece, not knowing that a $10,000 machine was sitting idle.
- Have regular stand-up meetings. Ask employees to give a brief summary of the work and what remains to be done, handle any coordination issues, and give any directions. Keep these

meetings short and to the point. You will learn much about your employees from these interactions.

- A 360-degree assessment where you take input from a large number of sources, including superiors, peers, subordinates, and customers when applicable, will provide useful information about your employees. This works better for relatively senior employees as well since input from subordinates can often be very illuminating.
- Use mission boards and whiteboards to mark targets and challenges so that they are visible to all employees, and everyone can be held accountable.
- Formal measurement processes emphasize the importance of the assessment process. Employees take these seriously.

In all cases, work out the important issues and discuss the points you wish to make with the employee concerned. Give all employees adequate opportunity to express their point of view. Each interaction can be a learning experience for you too.

23. Measuring Performance

A performance review is an important occasion that allows both employee and manager to establish realistic goals and expectations for the near future. Objective and healthy feedback will help your employee grow and contribute more to the company.

Managers often tend to sugarcoat problems out of hesitation or wanting to avoid unpleasant situations. While it may be important to maintain good working relationships, you will harm both your business and the employee by not being candid and open. If you do not discuss problem areas and work out their solutions, the problems will only fester and become larger with time.

During a review, focus on both the positive and the negative aspects of the employee's performance and bring out areas where improvement is required. You should also set goals and expectations for the future.

It is important to have objective, quantifiable criterion to measure performance. Typically, these fall into areas of quality, quantity, and time.

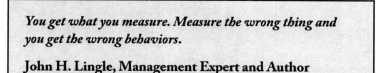

> *You get what you measure. Measure the wrong thing and you get the wrong behaviors.*
>
> **John H. Lingle, Management Expert and Author**

Considering **Quality** of work, you could be measuring and discussing the following factors:

- Customer satisfaction and feedback
- Any complaints
- Work output that must be redone (in percentage terms)
- Peer perception of job performance
- Adherence to procedures
- Budget management
- Attitude and behavior
- Percentage of leads that result in sales
- Consistency of quality

Be sure that you define quality norms well in advance so that all employees know what is expected of them.

When measuring **Quantity,** be careful to ensure that the quantity of work or output is qualitatively sound. The gadgets that an employee produces must be saleable. Sheer quantity without quality is only harming your business.

Measuring **Time**-related issues is equally important. Can you rely on the employee to get things done on time? Does the employee coordinate complex activities with peers and customers? Is the employee punctual? Do employees place company welfare above their own at least on some occasions?

24. Performance Evaluation

Evaluations are an important activity that either initiates corrective action or guides the employee to continue performing at a certain level. A good review can convert the process into a collaborative effort where everyone concerned gains.

To be able to tell employees whether or not they are doing a great job will largely depend on your understanding of the work they are doing. You must understand the job description well enough to be able to make such a determination. Once you are clear about the job content, you will be able to design criterion for measuring performance.

> *How you measure the performance of your managers directly affects the way they act.*
>
> **John Dearden, professor at Harvard Business School**

In essence, the evaluation process checks for three activities:

- Job Accountability—How closely has the employee met the requirements of the job?
- Goal Achievement—Assess whether or not the employee has met established goals.
- Additional Value Add—Check if the employee went beyond what was required and brought value to your business. Did the employee contribute in ways that were not expected? Has the employee shown willingness to walk the extra mile and give extra service both to your company and your customers? Does the employee fit in well with the organization, or does the employee cause friction among workers?

Performance evaluation is not a casual affair. You will give the process greater impact and value by being prepared yourself. All well-established companies must have a properly designed review form. Your employee must be given this form well before the review and asked to fill in the self-assessment section of the form and submit it before the review. In case of any doubt, discuss the employee with another supervisor to get a more objective view.

Other activities are shown below:

- Decide a place and time for the review. Ensure you will not be interrupted during this period.
- Prepare yourself by reading the self-appraisal and the job description and being thoroughly familiar with both. Determine if any part of the job description needs to be changed for the future.
- Review your notes on the employee's performance. Complete the evaluation form. Comment on an attribute if the employee is rated too high or too low in some field. Ensure that your comments are:
  - Objective and fair
  - Can quantify or qualify specific areas
  - Not general statements but specific observations
  - Relevant and meaningful
- Ensure that you cover the entire review period; guard against the effect of recent events
- An objective assessment will stand scrutiny and can be defended
- Evaluate all factors relevant to the employee

With this preparation, you now meet with the employee. Review the job description to see if any changes are required. This will also ensure that there is no ambiguity between what the duties involve as you see them and how the employee understands them.

You can next discuss the self-appraisal and the appraisal you have produced. This will bring out areas where you do not agree and you should be able to say why.

The discussion will then lead to goals set for the next assessment period and be able to incorporate any job content changes that may be necessary.

Once the process is over, you complete the documentation and send it for employee certification. Remember that certification is not an agreement, and the employee can add any comments to the evaluation.

The evaluation will be available to the employee after it is approved.

The Golden Rules

- Performance reviews are a frank and fair discussion of the employee's strengths and weaknesses.
- Help maintain open communication and enable discussion about other aspects of the job.
- Allow improvement to be planned and motivate the employee to do better.
- Improve relationships in the company.

Performance review checklist:

- Fix a date and time
- Select a suitable location
- Get the self-assessment form from the employee
- Prepare yourself by reading the job description and the self-appraisal; consult your notes
- Determine the strengths and weaknesses of the employee; make your notes
- Plan and conduct the review with maturity, fairness, and a positive attitude
- Summarize the situation and review the follow-up actions that the employee is required to take

If the review process is conducted well, you should be able to notice an immediate improvement in the areas you and the employee have identified.

25. Handling Poor Performance

In case you have any employees who are not living up to job expectations, there could be several reasons for unsatisfactory performance:

- They do not know what is expected of them
- They do not know how to perform the job
- They are not capable of performing the job
- They do not want to do the job

> *Performance stands out . . . Nonperformance can always be explained away.*
>
> **Harold S Geneen, CEO ITT 1959 - 77**

You would not want to keep incompetent or unwilling employees on your payroll. They cause a loss in terms of their own output, and they also affect other employees, who will notice that bad behavior or poor performance is being accepted, and it is only a matter of time before many of them follow suit.

26. Communication and Feedback

As soon as practical, you must give feedback to your employees about their standards of performance, which includes both good and bad news. The U.S. Department of Labor has stated that the number 1 reason for employees leaving a company is poor communication and a feeling that their efforts are not appreciated.

Giving feedback is an art you must develop. Your interest is only in the development of employees and improvement in their standards of work.

By giving your employees **positive feedback** (when deserved), you show them that:

- You are attentive to what they do and how they do it
- Their efforts are appreciated
- They are further encouraged to perform better
- Their actions are reinforced

Do not, however, go to the other extreme and give lavish, false praise. If you do this just as an attempt to create a good atmosphere, people will soon pay little attention to your remarks. Be fair and offer praise when it is truly deserved.

There are certain basic rules of feedback:

- Give positive feedback in public, negative feedback in private
- Be timely. Try to give positive feedback immediately after noticing a certain activity; give negative feedback within 24 hours. The difference is because you are giving positive strokes publicly, and you do not need to wait for a specific time.
- Focus on behavior, not the person. Instead of saying "you are habitually careless," say, "you have damaged the equipment."
- Be sure of your facts. Take some time to check in case you have any doubt.

Encourage your customers to give good feedback to your employees as well. If a customer is happy about a certain order and says so, introduce him to the employee who was instrumental in the success. This will give you a super-motivated employee. This is such a powerful way to motivate your staff that you must take advantage of every opportunity for such reinforcement.

On those occasions when your employee does not perform to your expectations, be quick to address the issue before it results in further damage. Essentially, employees fail for any of these six reasons:

- × They are unclear about the job
- × They are unclear about how to perform
- × They have a training gap
- × Conflicting priorities may prevent them from doing the job

× Something else appears to be more important
× They have an attitude problem

Once you have determined the core issue, you are ready to discuss the problem.

Tell the employee that you have identified a problem area in performance. Ask why the problem occurred. Together, you can now work out a plan to address the issue and ensure that the problem does not recur. It is best if the employee comes up with the solution since the employee will then be personally involved in the corrective action. Try to achieve this even if you have a ready-made solution available. The best action occurs when the person acknowledges both the problem and comes up with the solution.

> *The shortest word in the English language that contains the alphabets a b c d e f ? Feedback!*
>
> **Anonymous**

Here are some typical problems you could encounter:

× Absent while at work—chatting, flirting, or spending time on the Internet; there is an increasing trend of such behavior
× Poor involvement in safety—ensure that you have a safety manual and regularly cover the drills in it; do not condone safety violations since they have very serious repercussions
× A regular pattern of errors—check to determine if they are related
   × Do they occur at a certain time?
   × Do they occur on a particular task?
   × Does the employee realize the error?
   × Could confusion or noise or distractions be the cause?
× Missing deadlines—check for scheduling and overloading
× Causing workplace conflict—deal with this one quickly

27. Following Up on Performance

The process of employee performance improvement does not end with giving your employee meaningful and careful feedback. You need to follow up on the change in behavior and performance to be sure that it has had the desired impact.

You will need to follow up carefully yourself and make sure that the changes you discussed have become permanent. The effect of your counseling and the change will be better and bring more positive results if you make the employee participate in the process rather than you giving all the answers.

When faced with an underperforming employee, make sure that you have done the following:

- Established job performance standards and expectations
- Clearly stated standards and expectations
- Obtained receipts of communication (OK and understood)
- Provided adequate training
- Provided coaching
- Given the employee regular feedback
- Provided a mentor

If all this has been done but the employee is not coming up to your expectations, you need to sit down and devise a performance action plan.

When a convincing **Performance Action Plan** is drawn up between employee and manager, the employee will be accountable for the plan's success and will have an interest in making it succeed.

A sample performance review and action plan can be found in Appendix H.

Ensure that progress under the plan can be evaluated using the SMART criteria—Specific, Measurable, Accountable, Realistic, Timely.

Give the employee adequate time to achieve visible results. Continue to provide accurate feedback on performance.

If after adequate efforts the employee still continues to display poor results, you have two choices—either move the employee to a simpler job or plan a dismissal. The first option seldom works because no one likes to be brought down publicly.

We will discuss procedures to dismiss employees a little later.

28. Handling Complacency

Complacency can occur if employees are too settled and comfortable in their job. Lack of challenge in a job that has become routine is another major reason.

In an organization where employees are becoming complacent, we see the following characteristics develop:

- × Less communication between manager and employee
- × Employees work for short-term gains
- × Less daily monitoring and feedback
- × Managers also tend to wait for problems to occur rather than anticipate them
- × People tend to pass the buck and blame one another
- × Customer satisfaction suffers
- × Even though some employees may want to work, the culture prevents them from doing their best
- × People can be demoralized

> *The moment you start reducing expectations, you risk introducing complacency*
>
> **Peter Mandelson, British MP**

Your job as a manager is to ensure this does not happen. That does not mean that you keep people off balance and uncomfortable; some managers do try that with disastrous effects. You can break complacency by providing a degree of challenge in a job. If a job takes thirty minutes, challenge your staff to save five minutes on a regular basis. Ask if they can change the process to make the procedure more efficient or use fewer resources. Keep them thinking. And when you do get an employee to do something spectacular, remember the paragraphs on rewards and positive feedback.

Break monotony by well-planned activities and rotate employees between jobs wherever possible. Such changes also provide cross-training. Not only do your employees appreciate one another's work, you will also have a cross-trained employee should you have a shortage in another domain.

The Golden Rules

- Look out for complacency; this is when accidents occur.
- Keep challenging your employees in a constructive manner.
- Encourage them to make the work process more efficient.
- Break monotony.
- Encourage cross-training.

29. Managing Change

Let's face it. We all like certainty, and no one likes change—more so when the reasons for change are not made clear.

Your employees will not like change either. While you may have the most compelling reasons for the change, unless you get your employees on board, the change is not going to be successful.

When faced with a change situation, remember that the employee may not have the input you have and may be wondering why the change is needed. To get their support, you need to convince them.

Much research has gone into the subject of change management. Scores of people have received PhDs in this subject. But, basically, it all boils down to simple psychology.

Employees resist change because of clearly documented reasons:

- They do not understand what the change involves
- They do not understand how it will affect them
- They do not understand the reason behind the change

When you have to implement a change that is large and likely to cause worry, take the time to talk to your employees in detail. Speak to them in small groups so that you can talk to them individually and give them detailed reasons about the change and what it involves. Be sure to give them the opportunity to ask as many questions as they wish.

If your reasons are logical and convincing, these employees will spread the word and convince others.

The Golden Rules

- Understand that change makes people nervous.
- Employees need to be reassured that the change is not going to hurt them.
- They need to be convinced that the change is needed.

30. Pay and Performance

Pay and performance are closely linked because to a large extent one determines the other.

As we shall see elsewhere in this book, there is much involved in employee motivation besides pay. Nevertheless, employee compensation is one of the largest expenses of the company. It also has an important role in employee perceptions of the company since it sends a message about what standards of work and performance are desirable.

Compensation can also be an emotional issue with many people when you are assessing their self-worth in terms of a paycheck. Whether or not the company is fair to its employees will also depend on the company's salary structure.

As mentioned earlier, performance itself can be examined in three different areas:

- Job accountability—whether the employee is meeting the requirements that were described when the employee was hired
- Goal attainment—whether employees are able to meet their own goals
- Value-added functions, such as good communication, building relationships with clients, maintaining a positive attitude, and going out of the way to help the business

Compensation needs to be based on these three parameters and will also need to take into account the location of the business, the experience level of the employee, salary levels of similar employees in the company and in similar businesses in the vicinity. If the job is very specialized and critical to the company, this will also have an impact on the salary you offer.

Be extremely careful in deciding compensation. It is essential to be fair and to be visibly fair. Ensure that gender, race, sexual preference, religion, and nationality have nothing to do with deciding what you pay. As far as possible, be very consistent and transparent with your compensation plans. Used well, compensation can be a great motivator, but there are many other motivators that you will see later.

The Golden Rules

- There is much more to motivation than just pay.
- Ensure compensation has nothing to do with gender, race, sexual preference, religion, or nationality. When in doubt, imagine explaining your stand to a court.

31. Delegation

Successful managers are often masters of delegation. You can never be good at everything your business requires to be done. If you have chosen your employees with care and have trained them well, you should be able to delegate to them. Any executive who attempts to do everything himself will soon get caught in the details and will lose sight of the big picture.

> *We accomplish all that we do through delegation—either to time or to other people*
>
> **Stephen R Covey, Motivational Writer**

Many executives are afraid to let go and fear the loss of control and mistakes employees will make. But then you, too, could make mistakes. It is important to understand that while delegation gives you many benefits, the most important one is that you get time away from the grind to think constructively, and your employees can develop as well.

People feel good about being given a job they know is important. It tells them that you trust them and that you care about helping them grow even at the cost of some risk.

Wherever possible, delegate the entire job rather than bits and pieces. This allows your employees to take ownership of the entire job and take the praise or the flak.

Here are a few steps to ensure you delegate without surprises:

- Be very clear about what the job is and how it is to be done
- Brief your subordinate very clearly
- Make your requirements clear
- Have faith (perhaps the most difficult of all)
- Allow freedom to work; accept that different people do the same job differently
- Encourage your employees to take charge and solve the problem themselves rather than looking to you for guidance

- Keep track of what is happening, but don't breathe down their necks

How to judge if a job can be delegated to someone? Simple. Determine if it falls into one of the categories listed below:

- Tasks that need a skill level lower than yours
- Jobs that need a skill set you do not have
- Lower-priority jobs
- Jobs that other employees have been trained for

Then there are some jobs that cannot be delegated. See below for a list of how to decide:

- × Where the job involves giving bad news or decisions that will be opposed
- × When objectives are not defined and uncertainty is high
- × If something is going wrong and affects the company or department
- × When the risk of failure is high

In all the cases listed above, you are responsible. That is what leadership is all about.

The Golden Rules

- A successful manager will excel at delegation.
- You can delegate a job, but the responsibility stays with you.
- Do not delegate jobs that involve bad news or have a high degree of uncertainty.
- Do not delegate if the risk is high.

32. Discipline and Termination

Much as you'd hate it, this is also part of the job, and at some time or another you may be called upon to do.

> **Some people regard discipline as a chore. For me, it's a kind of order that sets me free to fly.**
>
> **Julie Andrews**

Several aspects are involved in discipline and termination. The disciplining process is not creating grounds for a dismissal; rather, it is attempting to correct the behavior that is causing a problem. If this happens, then you have succeeded in saving an employee's job. Other employees will also see the process and take note.

There is a human aspect to the process as well. You want to keep the procedure dignified and mature.

And, finally, there is a legal element. The actions you take could be challenged in court. You must take steps to ensure you follow the right procedures, and that adequate notice and support are given to the employee before any termination.

Disciplinary action could take the form of verbal counseling, which could be followed up with a written warning if no improvement occurs and more severe action if necessary.

A typical disciplinary process could take the form as shown in the table below.

Step	Action taken
1.	Verbal counseling. Record the event and the points discussed in the employee's file. Record data and time and people present.
2.	First written warning. Retain copy of all warnings in the employee's file.
3.	Second written warning followed (maybe) by a short suspension.

4.	Third written warning followed by (maybe) a longer suspension.
5.	Termination from service.

Warning notices are very important documents and will often be required to be produced in court. You must ensure that the employee is given adequate time between two such notices so that behavior can be changed and for results to be seen.

All warning letters or notices must follow certain guidelines. These are listed below.

- Always use the company letterhead.
- Never use email.
- The notice must relate to a specific incident. Mention the date, time, and what happened.
- Do not include several issues in one letter.
- Before issuing the notice, check the employee's documents carefully to ensure that the notice serial number is in correct sequence, and that the severity of the warning matches the offense.
- If you are suspending the employee, say so specifically and mention the exact dates from and to which you are suspending the employee.
- Obtain a signed receipt from the employee on a copy of the warning letter. In case the employee refuses to sign, record this fact on the copy and have another employee witness it.
- Follow legal advice in complex cases.

A sample warning notice is placed in Appendix I to this book.

Be prepared to follow through if you have given a final warning but another infraction occurs.

The Golden Rules

- Do not shy away from disciplining your workforce.
- The focus is on correction; you should attempt to correct and retain the employee.
- Do not lose your dignity.
- Ensure you are legally correct.
- Give adequate opportunity to correct.
- Follow through if required.

33. The Exit Procedure

The exit of an employee needs to be orderly and smooth. You must ensure that all login rights are revoked, access control cards are returned, and any non-disclosure agreements, noncompeting clauses, etc., are properly put into place. Also check that all documentation relating to taxation and benefits is complete and forwarded to the appropriate authorities.

It will help if you take the time to develop a comprehensive checklist so that important issues are not overlooked.

The Exit Interview

This is an important occasion when the exiting employee can give you very valuable input about you and your company. Take time to talk to the individual so that you get to know things that would otherwise not come to your attention.

Employees leaving of their own accord or retiring are often willing to give you very useful input provided you are receptive. This can often be an emotional encounter that you should respect.

In some cases of dismissal, it may not be possible or even desirable to hold an exit interview. Even then, ensure that exit procedures in terms of revoking privileges, return of access cards, etc., are fully followed. You could outsource this activity to a third party if the acrimony is excessive. Even in such cases, ensure that you complete all paperwork associated with benefits, insurance, etc., since you do not want to be legally liable at a later date.

The Golden Rules

- Keep exits smooth.
- Have a defined procedure to revoke rights, security permits, etc.
- The exit interview can give you valuable input.
- Ensure correct paperwork with benefits, insurance, etc.

Retaining Good Employees and Maintaining Relations

I t is not easy to find good employees, and we have seen how critical good employees are to a successful business. Getting great employees is hard work and can be very expensive. The next step is ensuring that they continue to work for you with their heart and soul and are not waiting for the right time to switch to one of your competitors.

The bad news is that in most cases management is most responsible for driving away good employees.

The good news is that there is much you can do to retain employees and build a happy, hardworking, and innovative team. Monetary compensation is but a small part of it. Much of your employee retention depends on the quality of communication with your employees.

34. Good Workplace Communication

A recent survey by Mercer Human Resource Consulting Company revealed that good communication in the workplace is a critical factor in an employee's decision to relocate. For those employees who said they were not kept informed by their company, a full 41% were contemplating switching jobs, and as many as 42% were dissatisfied.

These figures fell to 15% and 6% in companies where employees said communication was good.

Clarify Your Mission

You could call it a vision statement, a mission statement, or a set of goals. The term is unimportant. What is critical is that employees know very clearly what the company stands for, how it is moving toward its goals, and where the employee fits in.

Share Your Results

> *Good communication is as stimulating as black coffee and just as hard to sleep after.*
>
> **Anne Morrow Lindbergh**

In a number of cases, employees complain that they learn how their company is doing from reading the newspaper or other external resources. If you share this information with them *before* you send it to the press, not only will they feel they are a more important part of the company, but you will also find them performing better and understand the reasons why you (or the company) make certain decisions.

Share Success (and Defeats)

There will be a fair share of both. Sharing them with your employees will prepare them for the bad times and help them build on the good ones.

The Golden Rules

*   Communicate with your employees at every opportunity.

- Share your vision.
- Tell them the good and the bad; don't let rumors circulate.

35. Managing Employees

If you were to look at your employees in terms of their performance level, you could easily divide them into top-performing employees, average employees, and below-average employees.

Handling each type has peculiarities and specific methods. Using the wrong methods will certainly be counterproductive.

Top Employees

As their manager, it is your responsibility to ensure that your top employees stay with you for as long as you can manage it. You will do this by keeping them challenged and giving them opportunities to grow professionally. When you are really required to think outside the box, you need to ensure that your own goals and those of your employees coincide.

As said earlier, make sure that your goals are SMART—specific, measurable, achievable, realistic, and timely.

However, just because the employee is smart and hardworking, you still have to monitor and mentor. Your monitoring will be less apparent and more discrete, but you still need to do it. These employees are aware of their worth and need feedback just as other employees do.

Managers sometimes make the mistake of overpromising rewards to their top employees. Nothing can be less motivating than to lead someone to expect rewards and then let that person down. You can offer advanced training or more say in decision-making. Both of these are proven methods to increase an employee's self-confidence and morale.

Average Employees

You should be keenly interested in converting all your average employees into great ones. These employees are basically sound and competent. You just need to encourage them to develop their talents a little more and try a little harder.

Ensure that you make these employees strive just a little harder by presenting small challenges that stretch them a little beyond what they're doing now. Every time you make them take a step ahead of where they were before, you make them grow into better employees.

Do not hold back on positive feedback. People in this group are at times uncertain of their own self-worth and will do very well with positive input.

Difficult Employees

Recognizing such employees is simple. They are the ones who are complaining out loud to you or to anyone who will listen. Since this behavior can have adverse effects on your business and on other employees, it is not wise to ignore it.

In general, bad and destructive behavior has a tendency to spread. Once you allow one person to go rogue, many others on the fence will follow.

If there is a sudden deterioration in employee behavior, investigate immediately. There is always a reason and the faster you can discover and correct it the less the damage will result.

Do not use only secondhand sources to determine the problem. Investigate yourself and find out what is really going on.

Some simple warning signs you can look for include the following:

× Small groups that talk but stop when you pass
× A fixed group that gathers often
× Someone calling in sick more often than warranted
× Greater friction with coworkers
× Antagonism and aggression
× Frequent negative remarks
× Unwillingness to do anything extra
× Exhorting others to display similar behavior

Proper handling of such employees follows a few basic steps:

- Identify the problem—both the person and the behavior
- Let the person know that you are aware of the problem
- Tell the employee what will likely happen—both for that person and for the company
- Make your expectations clear
- Ask the person to present a plan for correcting the problem; review and confirm the plan
- Monitor progress

In some cases, you may have no option but to let the employee go. Before taking this drastic step, however, be sure you have made a genuine effort to sort out the difficulty. Problem employees are often capable and imaginative persons who can become very important contributors if handled well.

The Golden Rules

- Top employees look for opportunity.
- Top employees also need mentoring and feedback.
- Challenge average employees by giving them work that requires more work than usual.
- Provide plenty of positive feedback to average employees every time they grow a little.
- Keep a lookout for difficult employees.
- Correct difficult employees early.
- Monitor difficult employees closely.

36. Employee Motivation

> *Nothing great was ever achieved without enthusiasm.*
>
> **Ralph Waldo Emerson**

There are many other factors besides the paycheck that motivate employees to stay on and deliver better results. Motivation is an important subject in its own right, and much research has gone into how employees are kept motivated. We list some of the most important ones here.

- The challenge of the job
- The workplace environment
- Flexibility in the workplace
- Recognition
- Being part of a friendly and supportive team
- A fair workplace
- Good communication
- Other nonfinancial factors, such as
  - Personal growth
  - Career advancement opportunity
  - Flexible work schedule
  - Appreciation
  - Camaraderie

The Golden Rules

- Nonfinancial motivators are as important as financial ones.
- Use challenges, the workplace environment, and recognition to motivate your employees.
- Be fair.
- Have a great environment.
- Offer personal growth and appreciation.

37. Benefits and Perks

> *Far too many executives have become more concerned with the four Ps—Pay, Perks, Power, and Prestige rather than making profits for shareholders.*
>
> **T Boone Pickens, American business magnate and financier**

Benefits differ from other motivators in that they are not aligned to performance but are made available to every employee. These can include insurance, medical, sick leave, paid leave, overtime rates, retirement savings plans, and so on. These are made available to every employee who meets specified criteria, such as being with the company for more than a certain number of days or working more than a specified number of hours per week.

Whatever you do, ensure that the benefits criteria is available on the internal website (or manual) of the company, and that it is applied so fairly and transparently that if any employee were to calculate these, the value would not change. You will gain more overall by being fair than by giving too many benefits to a few star performers. You can use many other methods, but do not tinker with the benefits program.

Bonuses

A bonus is a form of performance-related pay, and there are advantages both for and against giving bonuses. While bonuses have a motivating effect on the person who gets it, there could be adverse reactions from those who don't. For this reason, many companies do not publicize the bonuses they pay. Others do, so you must really choose your own style, but here are the pros and cons:

Pros

- Assures employees that they are paid by objective standards instead of by whims and fancies of their supervisor
- Makes employer expectations clear
- Rewards high performance
- Bonuses work well with jobs that can be easily measured, such as production on the shop floor

Cons

- × Reduces a complex job to a single measure of performance
- × May force multiple employees to compete for getting business—may vitiate working environment
- × Economic slowdown may penalize employee for inability to sell
- × Can jeopardize safety and other norms because some people may resort to taking shortcuts to increase production
- × Does not work with jobs where several people are involved in eventual success
- × Since measurement of productivity is difficult in some other jobs, bonuses may not work for jobs involving knowledge and decision-making skills

Some examples of circumstances where bonuses could be paid:

- Salespersons exceeding quotas
- Innovations for improving processes and increasing savings
- Attracting new customers
- Exceeding collections
- Finishing projects ahead of time or under budget
- Working substantially more than required

You will need to decide in advance what the bonus amount can be and allocate accordingly. Once again, bonus guidelines must be decided well in advance and made very clear to all employees. Being fair is critical.

Nonmonetary Awards

Numerous surveys have shown that employees want recognition and appreciation more than anything else.

The rewards must be carefully chosen. They must meet the following criteria:

- Should be consistent with the corporate message and company goals
- Be very clearly tied to job performance
- Be very fairly selected
- Be distinct from pay and other privileges

Why not ask your employees themselves how they want to be recognized? You will get many great ideas and suggestions. Make sure that the award does not become routine or it will lose its value. There is no necessity to declare an employee of the month if that has not clearly been the case.

Here are some ideas you can use to appreciate your employees:

- Give an extra day off
- Gift cards or coupons
- Tickets to a show or a game
- Pinning a congratulatory poster on the office notice board
- Gift a monogrammed mug filled with candy
- Gifts such as laptop bags, briefcases, etc.

The Golden Rules

- Benefits are available in equal measure to all employees.
- Make the benefit criteria absolutely fair and transparent.
- Bonuses are performance related.
- All rewards must be clearly tied to job performance.
- Nonmonetary rewards work well too.

Information Technology & Human Resource Management

38. Information Technology in the Workplace

> *Information technology and business are becoming inextricably interwoven. I don't think anybody can talk meaningfully about one without talking about the other.*
>
> **Bill Gates**

There is no denying the importance of information technology to today's businesses. As far back as 1977, a study estimated that 47 percent of American workers were engaged in information-based activities. This number would be far greater now. Every workplace today needs its workers to use basic information technology tools and have access to the Internet.

This creates unique opportunities and challenges. Let us look at the opportunities first:

- Your workforce is now increasingly mobile. Employees can stay connected with the office wherever they go.

- Telecommuting has become a reality. You can permit a substantial number of employees to work away from the office. A study has shown that 91 percent of organizations have at some time or another permitted their employees to work from home. Advantages include the following:
  - Productivity improvement
  - Reduced absenteeism
  - Improved morale and employee retention
  - Reduced cost of office space
  - Reduced cost of office relocation
  - Virtual teams can be formed across continents, bringing new and great capabilities to the workplace

There are a number of disadvantages as well. Knowing these allows you to avoid them:

- × Security issues
- × Loss of teamwork—even though occasional office visits are planned, some jobs require closer teamwork and cannot be open to telecommuting
- × Supervision and issues with performance evaluation
- × Issues with workload distribution
- × Customer acceptance

Many business owners and managers lag in this area due to a lack of IT knowledge and skills. In today's lean and mean times, IT gives managers the edge to minimize cost and improve efficiencies.

The Golden Rules

- No modern business can neglect IT in the workplace and hope to thrive.
- Telecommuting brings many benefits.
- Using virtual teams brings opportunities that were not available before.
- Consider customer needs when implementing telecommuting options.

39. IT in HR Administration

From a purely administrative point of view, IT systems can assist in the following activities:

- Payroll
- Work/Time management
- Appraisal performance
- Benefits administration
- HR management information system
- Recruiting
- Performance record
- Employee self-service

Many of these can be fully automated. For example, if you install a clocking in-and-out system in your workplace, it can be linked straight to your payment software to enter most of the data about pay calculations. Such a system keeps attendance records and provides an input to the pay and allowances system. A large number of automation products are currently available.

Modern IT developments are moving to using cloud computing and collaborative software. In cloud computing, very large data centers on the Internet are used to provide servers that are used by companies to run their software applications, databases, and storage. This technology removes the need for individual companies to manage their server farms and data centers, and the cost of computing is dramatically reduced. In cloud computing, there are no fixed costs for the services you hire. You only pay for how long you actually use the service. This lowers costs further. Even small companies can use the same top-end software as a Fortune 100 company.

Collaborative software allows users in different locations to work on the same task simultaneously, so if one user has opened a word processor document, another user somewhere else with the correct authorizations can work with the first user.

The Golden Rules

- A small company can overcome its shortcomings and compete against much larger companies by using IT imaginatively.
- IT assists HR management enormously by making processes faster, more accurate, and accessible.

40. Major Software in Use

With the advent of modern technology, many changes have occurred in the workplace. Efficiencies have increased, and many things that were not considered possible a couple of decades ago are now commonplace.

In this section, we examine a few of the major software classes and give you brief details about them.

Project Management software—ZOHO is one of the better-known project management software on the market. Both free and paid versions are available. You can find it at http://www.zoho.com/projects/. This is a fully web-based project management application that does not require any IT infrastructure at the user end other than an Internet connection and a web browser. Setting up is instantaneous.

ZOHO offers an interactive timeline view of your ongoing projects. You can see them in a number of different views and change the duration of various projects as required with ease.

A large number of report formats are available, and users can also customize and build their own formats. Reports can be exported to a number of formats such as pdf or MS Excel.

ZOHO allows you to manage your email from the application itself, and messages about projects and their timelines are automatically generated and sent to the persons you designate. This ensures that communication is automatic and everyone in the pipeline is kept informed.

Videoconferencing—With modern computer networks, it is now possible to easily transfer video all over the world in real time. A large number of video-conferencing solutions, both hardware and software based, are available with choice, depending on the price you are willing to pay. You can even go in for very low cost or free solutions such as Skype.

Task Managers—Task management software helps workers and managers to be organized, productive, and more operational through automated and collaborative tools that smooth the workflow in the office and help increase productivity. It has been calculated that once employees learn to use Task Managers well, their efficiency would increase by up to 150%. A good task manager (among many that are available) is Producteev, available at www.producteev.com

Survey Gizmo—A number of survey tools that automate the collection and presentation of data are available. One such tool is Survey Gizmo. This and similar types of tools allow you to create a customized survey with hundreds of questions that can be distributed online to a large number of responders. The tool supports managing responses and converting them into reports that analyze the data and update a website automatically.

LogMeIn—A number of applications allow you to work collaboratively with your coworkers on the network. LogMeIn is one such application. It gives you the following functionality:

- Access Your Personal Computer
- Access Your Computer from Your Mobile Device
- Virtually Network Your Devices Together
- Control Your Remote Desktop for Free
- Support Friends' and Family's Computers
- Back Up Your Computer Files and Folders
- Support Remote Computers and Smartphones
- Access Work Computers
- Connect Devices to Private Networks
- Manage Servers and Workstations
- Deliver Access, Management, and Networking as a Service
- Back Up Remote Computer Data

Team Viewer is software similar to LogMeIn.

Office Productivity Software—Nine out of ten persons in an office will probably be using some kind of office application at work. These comprise the following main program types:

- Word processors
- Spreadsheets
- Presentation programs
- Database management systems
- Personal information managers
- Schedulers and organizers

The following characteristics also make productivity software unique:

- Used almost daily by large numbers of users.
- The feature set is relatively static and offers a stable environment for most users. Even inexperienced users have a shallow learning curve.
- Data is stored in standard formats and can be easily shared among different programs (for example, rich text files, text data, and csv files).
- An increasing amount of interapplication communication. While this is transparent to most users, it greatly adds to the ease of work.

Some commonly used office automation software includes the Zoho Office Suite and Google Docs. These are available at http://www.zoho.com/ and https://docs.google.com/ respectively.

41. Attendance and Time Policy

Every business is interested in getting a fair deal from its employees. Toward that end, many businesses go in for an automated attendance tracking and management solution.

The problem with using punch cards and similar devices in the past was that there was a risk (often real) of buddy punching. Modern biometric devices eliminate that altogether.

Solutions interface directly with the payroll software so that in most cases calculation of pay is automatic. You can still control items such as overtime and any special payments or allowances.

There are issues with clocking time to ensure that workers do not clock in too early or clock out too late, as this will affect their overtime. At the same time, if you allow people to clock in only at 8 AM (or any other specified time), then you will end up with a long line of people waiting to clock in.

A good clocking solution has small relaxation in clocking times (which you control) so that people getting in or out +/– 5 minutes of the correct time are booked as going on the right time.

You may have some convincing to do if you are putting in a clocking system for the first time. You need to talk to your employees to convince them that deployment of such a system is not because you don't trust them but is being installed to ease your job of payroll creation and meeting regulatory compliance. And this is largely true. Using such automation means you will be able to get much greater accuracy into your payroll services.

A sample overtime form is available in <u>Appendix J</u>.

42. Need for IT/Internet Policy

An Internet usage policy is an important document in any organization. This is both an HR and an IT issue, and collaboration between them will produce a policy that makes sense and works well for both the company and the individual. The policy will ensure that threats from the Internet are reduced and controlled, individuals work as they are expected to, and that there are no legal issues emerging from their use of the Net.

If the policy is explained correctly, employees will know the reasons why they should not load just any software of their choice onto their PCs that will have an impact on the company network. There is also a difference between work and personal use as well as many security issues resulting from access to networking sites and personal email. Also important is the issue of slacking off on company time, which the Internet certainly promotes.

Internet usage policy has to be tailor-made for each organisation because it is specific to each, and there is no "one size fits all."

When it comes to policy implementation, action needs to be taken if there is continuous violation. A graded method of enforcement will be needed—maybe start with a verbal caution and move all the way up to the ultimate corrective action. Employees must know that the policy is firm and that there will be no exceptions; otherwise, the policy may end up becoming a joke.

The policy is best implemented by using automated monitoring tools, which ensure the lowest cost of monitoring and the fairest results.

A well-drafted, comprehensive IT policy must include the following aspects:

- Software authorized to be used. It must be made clear that besides the listed software, any other software will require permission to be loaded onto office PCs.
- Internet usage—must be restricted to office-related work only.
- Specific orders against pornography and nonbusiness use.
- Email usage—must include a specific statement saying all email through this system is business property and will be archived and scanned periodically.

Ensure that the employee is given a copy of the manual on day 1 at the workplace and obtain a written acknowledgment for your records.

At the same time, be practical about it. You don't want to be too intrusive if a person surfs the Net once in a while on a nonbusiness-related subject. Separate the time wasters from the occasional violators when you decide to initiate action.

The Golden Rules

- A clear IT policy is essential.
- Ensure new employees get to know the policy on the first day of work.
- Legal precedence exists for employers to monitor email and computer usage.

A Sample Internet Policy is placed in <u>Appendix K</u>

43. Monitoring Devices in the Workplace

In general, the following five main reasons exist for monitoring employees in the workplace:

- Ensuring legal compliance—for example, in telemarketing companies, it may be required to record the conversation between the worker and the client.
- Liability—the company can be held liable for certain acts, such as harassment or hostility. It helps if a record is available.
- Recorded data can be reviewed to improve employee performance.
- Evidence shows that employees waste less time if they are aware they are being watched.
- Security of equipment and intellectual property improves.

Just as good fences make better neighbors by laying down clearly defined limitations, clearly announced security policies are helpful in ensuring that your employees know what is acceptable and what is not.

Security devices could be mentioned here—control over rewritable media in case you are a company where intellectual property is a key asset (e.g., a software development house). Other systems could be monitoring of photocopiers, printers, scanners, and network traffic.

Where physical assets have to be protected, closed-circuit cameras and radio tagging of devices may have to be carried out.

What's important is announcing very clearly what is acceptable behavior and what is not. If you want to ensure that no employee is to take confidential company documents home without written authorization, your employees must know that, and you must have the demonstrated capability to catch offenders.

Section 6

HR & Labor Laws

44. Labor Laws in the USA

The content for this section is from the U.S. Department of Labor website, and you should refer to this site as a first source of laws on how to manage your human resources. Remember that the laws ensure that workers get a fair deal and that they are not exploited or discriminated against in the workplace. It is the responsibility of every manager to be acquainted with these. Ignorance as they say is no excuse.

Broadly, these relate to the following subheads (content from Department of Labor website www.dol.gov). It is strongly recommended that managers visit this excellent resource for information.

Wages—The Department of Labor enforces the Fair Labor Standards Act (FLSA), which sets basic minimum wage and overtime pay standards. These standards are enforced by the Department's Wage and Hour Division.

Workers who are covered by the FLSA are entitled to a minimum wage of not less than $7.25 per hour effective July 24, 2009. Overtime pay at a rate of not less than one and one-half times their regular rate of pay is required after 40 hours of work in a workweek. Certain exemptions apply to specific types of businesses or specific types of work.

The FLSA does not, however, require severance pay, sick leave, vacations, or holidays.

Hours—The Fair Labor Standards Act (FLSA) does not limit the number of hours per day or per week that employees aged 16 years and older can be required to work. For covered, nonexempt employees, the Fair Labor Standards Act (FLSA) requires overtime pay at a rate of not less than one and one-half times an employee's regular rate of pay after 40 hours of work in a workweek. Some exceptions to the 40 hours per week standard apply under special circumstances to police officers and firefighters employed by public agencies and to employees of hospitals and nursing homes.

Some states also have enacted overtime laws. Where an employee is subject to both state and federal overtime laws, the employee is entitled to overtime according to the higher standard (i.e., the standard that will provide the higher rate of pay).

Workplace Safety & Health—The Occupational Safety and Health (OSH) Act is administered by the DOL's Occupational Safety and Health Administration (OSHA). Safety and health conditions in most private industries are regulated by OSHA or OSHA-approved state systems. Nearly every employee in the nation comes under OSHA's jurisdiction with some exceptions, such as miners, some transportation workers, many public employees, and the self-employed. In addition to the requirements to comply with the regulations and safety and health standards contained in the OSH Act, employers subject to the Act have a general duty to provide work and a workplace free from recognized, serious hazards.

Workers' Compensation—The Department of Labor's Office of Workers' Compensation Programs (OWCP) administers four major disability compensation programs, which provide wage replacement benefits, medical treatment, vocational rehabilitation, and other benefits to federal workers or their dependents when those workers are injured at work or acquire an occupational disease.

> *An employee's motivation is a direct result of the sum of interactions with his or her manager.*
>
> **Bob Nelson**

Employee Benefits—Most private sector health plans are covered by the Employee Retirement Income Security Act (ERISA). Among other things, ERISA provides protections for participants and beneficiaries in employee benefit plans (participant rights), including providing access to plan information.

The Department of Labor's Employee Benefits Security Administration (EBSA) is responsible for administering and enforcing these provisions of ERISA. Click on the agency to find out more about the agency's program. As part of carrying out its responsibilities, the agency provides consumer information on health plans as well as compliance assistance for employers, plan service providers, and others to help them comply with ERISA.

Unions & Their Members—The Department of Labor's Office of Labor-Management Standards (OLMS) is the federal agency responsible for administering and enforcing most provisions of the Labor-Management Reporting and Disclosure Act of 1959 (LMRDA), which directly affects millions of people throughout the United States. The law was enacted to ensure basic standards of democracy and fiscal responsibility in labor organizations representing employees in private industry.

The major provisions of LMRDA are:

- A "bill of rights" for union members;
- Requirements for reporting and disclosure of financial information and administrative practices by labor unions;

- Requirements for reporting and disclosure by employers, labor relations consultants, union officers and employees, and surety companies, when they engage in certain activities;
- Rules for establishing and maintaining trusteeships;
- Standards for conducting fair elections of union officers; and
- Safeguards for protecting union funds and assets.

Retirement Plans, Benefits, and Savings—A pension plan is an employee benefit plan established or maintained by an employer or by an employee organization (such as a union), or both, that provides retirement income or defers income until termination of covered employment or beyond. There are a number of different types of retirement plans, including the 401(k) plan and the traditional pension plan, known as a defined benefit plan.

Most private sector pension plans are covered by the Employee Retirement Income Security Act (ERISA). Among other things, ERISA provides protections for participants and beneficiaries in employee benefit plans, including providing access to plan information. Also, those individuals who manage plans (and other fiduciaries) must meet certain standards of conduct under the fiduciary responsibilities specified in the law.

The Family and Medical Leave Act—Leave benefits allow employees to take time off from work. The extent of the leave and whether it is paid in whole, in part, or not at all is generally a matter of agreement between an employer and an employee (or the employee's representative). Certain types of leave are required by law, whereas other types are voluntary incentives provided by employers. The following subtopics (links provided) give more detailed information:

- Family & Medical Leave
- Funeral Leave
- Government Contracts
- Holidays
- Jury Duty

- <u>Personal Leave</u>
- <u>Sick Leave</u>
- <u>Vacations</u>

The Department of Labor enforces the Fair Labor Standards Act (FLSA). The public often thinks that the FLSA regulates "leave benefits." In fact, there are a number of employment practices that FLSA does not regulate. For example, it does not require:

- Vacation, holiday, severance, or sick pay.
- Meal or rest periods, holidays off, or vacations.
- Premium pay for weekend or holiday work.
- Pay raises or fringe benefits.
- Discharge notice, reason for discharge, or immediate payment of final wages to terminated employees.

Detailed data about any of these can be found at http://www.dol.gov. It is strongly recommended that all managers have at least a working knowledge of these laws. If you ever have to act urgently in a situation where you are not clear about the exact legal status of a situation, the best advice this book can offer is—

- Work with the best interests of the employee in mind
- Be fair
- Follow a totally nondiscriminatory approach to handling your staff

APPENDICES

Sample Job Description

Job Description Template:

Job Title:	
Classification:	
Department/ Division:	
Location:	
Pay Grade:	

Working Conditions:

Tasks:

Reports to:

Minimum Requirements:

Education	
Experience	
Training	
Physical attributes and capabilities	
Certificate/Licenses Required	
Skills required	
Computer knowledge	

Language requirements:

Writing	
Reading	
Speaking	

Sample Job Description:

Job Title	Financial Planning Sales
Classification	Full-Time Exempt Employee
Department/ Division	Financial Product/Western Regional
Location	Orange County California
Pay Grade	(Base + Commission)

Working Conditions:

- Work in high-volume sales office
- Be able to man a workstation for prolonged periods of time
- Be able to travel to client locations 25 percent of the time

Tasks:

- Research and create targeted new client lists within Orange County California territory
- Make initial contact with potential clients
- Performs routine and regular follow-up with potential clients
- Performs routine and regular follow-up with former clients
- Visits potential clients and makes sales presentations
- Closes sales
- Maintains regular record reporting sales activities

Reports to:

- Reports to regional sales manager
- Has nobody directly reporting to this position
- Required to participate in Annual Sales Meeting

Minimum Requirements:

Education	Bachelor's Degree in business, finance, or accounting or five years' experience and High School Diploma. Bachelor's Degree preferred
Experience	Minimum three years in a similar position
Training	ABC Financial Planning—Level 3 or higher
Physical attributes and capabilities	Healthy, capable of driving long distances, be able to handle sample packets weighing up to 20 lbs.

Certificate/Licenses required	CFP—Certified Financial Planner California Driver's License
Skills required	Fearless cold caller, 250+ outbound calls per week Ability to close a sale Adapt to changing financial conditions and meet customer expectations
Computer knowledge	Windows operating system MS Office—Word, Excel, and PowerPoint Constant Contact or other Customer Relations Management Software

Languages requirement:

Writing	English
Reading	English
Speaking	English, Spanish

Appendix B

Sample Job Application Form

Instructions: Print clearly in black or blue ink. Answer all questions. Sign and date the form.

PERSONAL INFORMATION:

First Name _____

Middle Name _____

Last Name _____

Street Address

_____

City, State, ZIP Code

_____

Phone Number

(___) _____

Are you eligible to work in the United States?

Yes _____ No _____

If you are under age 18, do you have an employment/age certificate?

Yes _____ No _____

Have you been convicted of or pleaded no contest to a felony within the last five years?

Yes _____ No _____

If yes, please explain:

POSITION/AVAILABILITY:

Position Applied For

_____

Days/Hours Available

Monday _____

Tuesday _____

Wednesday _____

Thursday _____

Friday _____

Saturday _____

Sunday _____

Hours Available: from _____ to _____

What date are you available to start work?

_____

EDUCATION:

Name and Address of School, Degree/Diploma, Graduation Date

_____

_____

_____

_____

Skills and Qualifications: Licenses, Skills, Training, Awards

_____

_____

EMPLOYMENT HISTORY:

Present Or Last Position:

Employer:

_____

Address:

_____

Supervisor:

_____

Phone: _____

Ali Asadi, MBA, MA (IT)

Email: _____

Position Title: _____

From: _____ To: _____

Responsibilities:

_____

_____

Salary: _____

Reason for Leaving:

_____

Previous Position:

Employer:

_____

Address:

_____

Supervisor:

_____

Phone: _____

Email: _____

Position Title: _____

From: _____ To: _____

Responsibilities:

_____

_____

Salary: _____

Reason for Leaving:

_____

May We Contact Your Present Employer?

Yes _____ No _____

References:

Name/Title Address Phone

_____

_____

_____

I certify that information contained in this application is true and complete. I understand that false information may be grounds for not hiring me or for immediate termination of employment at any point in the future if I am hired. I authorize the verification of any or all information listed above.

Signature _____

Date _____

Appendix C

Sample Evaluation Sheet

An applicant assessment form you could typically use is shown below. Using this theme, you could vary it to suit your particular requirements.

Applicant Assessment Form

Date	
Position applied for	
Applicant	
Interviewed By	

Rating Scale Values

1 = Unacceptable   2 = Below Average   3 = Acceptable
4 = Above Average   5 = Excellent

Sample Criteria	Applicant's Rating	Comment
Attitude		
Rapport/Confidence displayed		
Appearance		
Work History		
Ability to make judgments		
Education & Licenses		
Knowledge & Skills		
Language Proficiency		
Total		

Remarks

Record of Reference Checks

Name of Candidate _____

Position applied for _____

Title _____

Salary Grade _____

Name of Reference _____

Company _____

Rating Scale Values

1 = Unacceptable   2 = Below Average   3 = Acceptable
4 = Above Average   5 = Excellent

Factor	Marks by reference provider	Comments
Quality of work		
Volume of work		
Attitude to work		
Attitude toward coworkers		
Management/ Supervisory practices		
Subordinates' opinion of candidate		
Attendance and punctuality		
Promotions and awards		

Person conducting interview

_____

Signature _____

Date _____

Sample Job Offer letter

Name and Address

Date

Dear Mr./Miss/Mrs./Ms. (Name):

Congratulations! We are pleased to confirm that you have been selected to work for (Company/Division/Department). We are delighted to make you the following job offer.

The position we are offering is that of (Job Title) at a salary/wage of (salary/hourly rate) per (year/month/ week/hour). This position reports to (Title and name of Supervisor). Your working hours will be from (state working hours) and/or (normal workdays). This is a permanent/ seasonal/contract/casual) position. (If this is a contract position, state expected length of term.)

Benefits information if relevant to the position:

Vacation	-	__ weeks per annum
Probation (or Provisional) Period	-	from (dd/mm/yy) to (dd/mm/yy)

Employee Benefits Include: -   MSP
                              -    Group Insurance
                              -    Short/Long-Term Disability
                              -    Dental Care
                              -    Health Care

We would like for you to start work on (state desired date) at (state start time). Please report to (name of person to see on start date) for documentation and orientation. If this date is not acceptable, please contact me immediately.

Please sign the enclosed copy of this letter and return it to me by (specify date) to indicate your acceptance of this offer.

We are confident you will be able to make a significant contribution to the success of our (Company/Division/Department), and we look forward to working with you.

Sincerely,

(Name of person authorized to make job offer)
(Position)
(Company)

I accept the offer as outlined above.

(Name) _____   <u>Date</u>

Thank You Letter To All Unsuccessful Applicants

(Date)

(Applicant Name)
(Address)

Dear (Applicant Name),

Thank you for your recent inquiry about employment opportunities with **(Company Name)**.

At this time, however, we do not have any openings that match your skills and abilities. Furthermore, as a matter of policy in response to federal record-keeping requirements, we do not retain unsolicited résumés.

We hope to hear from you again, though, when a specific position for which we have listed and/or advertised is open. All of our open positions are listed on our website, **(web address of Company Name);** we also often advertise in newspapers, trade publications, and on various career websites.

In the meantime, we wish you success in your search for challenging and rewarding employment.

Sincerely,

(Name of Human Resources Representative)
(Title of Human Resources Representative)

(Company Name)

Appendix G

Sample Employee Evaluation Form

EMPLOYEE SELF-EVALUATION

EMPLOYEE NAME: _____

DATE: _____

EVALUATOR: _____

1. What were your principal accomplishments in your areas of responsibility since your last evaluation?

_____
_____
_____
_____
_____
_____

2. Within the areas of your responsibility, what are things you could improve or build upon?

_____
_____
_____
_____
_____
_____

3. Having reviewed your position description, do your areas of responsibility apply to this position? If certain areas do not, what adjustments do you feel should be made?

_____

_____

_____

_____

_____

_____

4. What aspects of the operations are you most satisfied with?

_____

_____

_____

_____

_____

_____

5. What aspects of the operations are you least satisfied with?

_____

_____

_____

_____

_____

_____

6. How do you feel about your career development with the company?

_____

_____

_____

_____

_____

_____

7.   Where do you see yourself two years from now?

_____

_____

_____

_____

_____

_____

Once this self-evaluation has been reviewed by the employee and evaluator, it should be attached to the employee's Performance Appraisal.

PERFORMANCE EVALUATION FORM

Employee: ———————————— Position: ——————————

Supervisor: ——————————— Department: ————————

Date: ———————————————— Time in ————————————

Position: ————————————————————————————

SECTION I—GENERAL PERFORMANCE STANDARDS

Consider each standard separately. Mark an X in the appropriate box that most reflects the evaluator's response. A substandard performance rating on any performance standard must be supported by specific comment in the space provided. Use additional sheets if necessary.

JOB KNOWLEDGE, SKILLS, AND ABILITIES: The employee demonstrates the knowledge, skills, and abilities necessary to perform work satisfactorily.

Does not have the basic knowledge, skills, and abilities to perform work satisfactorily.	Has the basic knowledge, skills, and abilities to perform work satisfactorily.	Has exceptional knowledge, skills, and abilities to perform work.

COMMENTS:

2. QUALITY OF WORK: The employee demonstrates accuracy, attention to detail, and effectiveness in completion of work.

Work is sometimes inaccurate or incomplete; fails to meet departmental standards.	Work is usually accurate and thorough; work meets departmental standards.	Work is consistently of excellent quality, accuracy, and detail.

COMMENTS:

3. PRODUCTIVITY: Employee performs work with efficiency, consistency, and timeliness.

Works slower than expected; work is of substandard consistency and timeliness.	Completes work on time, with consistency and efficiency; meets departmental standards.	Completes work quickly, often ahead of schedule; effectively prioritizes work; exceeds departmental standards.

COMMENTS:

4. RELIABILITY: The employee is dependable and conscientious in performing work and willing to accept responsibilities.

Sometimes is not dependable and conscientious in performing work; unwilling to accept responsibilities.	Consistently dependable and conscientious; usually accepts responsibilities; meets departmental standards.	Extremely dependable; follows through promptly on all tasks; accepts responsibilities; exceeds job goals; shows high level of initiative.

COMMENTS:

5. COMMUNICATION: The employee demonstrates the appropriate level of written and verbal communication skills necessary to satisfactorily perform the job.

Communication skills impair work performance.	Has the required communication skills and is effective in the position; meets departmental standards.	Has excellent communication skills; very effective in verbal and written interactions.

COMMENTS:

6. WORK RELATIONSHIPS: The employee is able to maintain effective and productive working relationships with fellow employees, supervisors, and the public.

Has trouble getting along with other employees, supervisors, and the public.	Has a generally positive approach in assisting others; maintains effective working relationships; meets departmental standards.	Exceeds departmental standards; highly cooperative; works hard to promote positive work relationships.

COMMENTS:

7. SAFETY: The employee adheres to rules and regulations to ensure safety standards are met.

Fails to follow safety rules and regulations; falls below departmental standards.	Follows safety rules and meets departmental standards.	Exceeds departmental standards for safety.

COMMENTS:

JOB PERFORMANCE STANDARDS

This section is designed to be "job specific." Refer to the "Job Performance Standards" of the employee's position description. Briefly list the major job duties specifically related to the performance of this job.

BELOW STANDARDS: Job performance generally falls below standards required for the position.

MEETS STANDARDS: Job performance satisfactorily meets the requirements for the position.

EXCEEDS STANDARDS: Job performance consistently exceeds the standards for the position.

	BELOW STANDARD	MEETS STANDARD	EXCEEDS STANDARD
JOB PERFORMANCE STANDARDS 1. COMMENTS:			
2. COMMENTS:			
3. COMMENTS:			
4. COMMENTS:			
5. COMMENTS:			

SECTION III—OVERALL WORK PERFORMANCE: Check the standard that matches the employee's OVERALL work performance. An overall work performance rating that does not meet "Job Requirements" requires specific explanation in the comment section. Explanation must include the specific job performance areas requiring improvement. Attach additional sheets as necessary.

Performance needs improvement to meet Job Requirements.	Performance meets Job Requirements	Performance exceeds Job Requirements.

COMMENTS:

SECTION IV—EMPLOYEE COMMENTS: Comments are encouraged—either agreeing, disagreeing, or acknowledging the supervisor's evaluation. Attach additional information if needed.

Supervisor's
signature: _____
Date: _____

Employee's
signature: _____
Date: _____

Chief Administrator's
signature: _____
Date: _____

NOTE: By signing this form, the employee acknowledges only that this evaluation was discussed and the employee has received a copy. The employee's signature does not signify agreement with the evaluation.

Appendix H

Sample of Employee Performance Improvement Plan

Performance Issues	Standard Required	Action and Support Given	Dates & Timelines	Outcomes
Development needs	Performance Requirements	Training or educational program, mentoring activity to develop/ improve skill performance.	List action timeline and reassessment date.	Results and/or accomplishments and related completion date

Sample of Warning Letter to Employee

(To be on official letterhead of company)

To:

From:

Date:

Re: Written Reprimand for _____

This is an official written reprimand for your failure to

_____
_____
_____
_____

You have received verbal counseling for similar behavior on several past occasions, but such counseling is not having the impact that had been expected. Consequently, this written reprimand is being given to you to remind you that _____ (enter the activity being done poorly) is a core requirement of your job description.

Continuing this behavior will lead to disciplinary action that could include job termination.

A copy of this written reprimand will be placed in your official personnel file.

Signature:

Supervisor Name:

Date:

Receipt of Written Reprimand

I acknowledge receipt of this written reprimand. My acknowledgment does not necessarily signify my agreement with its contents. I understand that a copy of this written reprimand will be placed in my official personnel file. I also understand that I have the right to prepare a written response that will be attached to the original written reprimand in my file.

Signature:

Employee Name:

Date:

Sample of Overtime Form

OVERTIME CONFIRMATION FORM

No	Date	T	Actual		Total Hours	Job Description	Sign	Name	Comment/ Remark
			Start	End					

T: N—Normal day   H—Holiday   R—Rest day

Note—This form must be completed and signed during the OT by the person who requested the OT. If the worker is NOT in the specified location for OT, DO NOT sign this form and please note this in the remark/comment column.

Appendix K

Sample of Internet Usage Policy

Internet usage policy

This Sample Internet Usage Policy applies to all employees of [Company name]. Use of the Internet by employees is encouraged and permitted for official business use, but all employees must adhere to the usage policies given below. Violation will result in disciplinary and/or legal action up to and including termination of employment. Employees may also be held personally responsible for damages caused by any violations of this policy. By signing below, you acknowledge receipt and confirm that you understand and agree to abide by the policy.

Internet usage

Employees are expected to use the Internet responsibly and productively. Internet access is limited to job-related activities only, and personal use is not permitted

All data received using this computer will be treated as company property. It may be archived and stored and used later. All email is subject to archival, monitoring or review by, and/or disclosure to, someone other than the recipient. It is therefore subject to disclosure for legal reasons or to other appropriate third parties. The company reserves the right to monitor Internet traffic.

Emails sent via the company email system should not contain content that is deemed to be offensive. This includes, though is not restricted to, the use of vulgar or harassing language/images.

All sites and downloads may be monitored and/or blocked if they are deemed to be harmful and/or not productive to business. The installation of any software not approved by the company is strictly prohibited.

Unacceptable use of the Internet by employees includes, but is not limited to the following:

- × Access to sites that contain obscene, hateful, pornographic, unlawful, violent, or otherwise illegal material
- × Sending or posting discriminatory, harassing, or threatening messages or images on the Internet or via [Company name] email service
- × Using computers to perpetrate any form of fraud and/or software, film, or music piracy
- × Stealing, using, or disclosing someone else's password without authorization
- × Downloading, copying, or pirating software and electronic files that are copyrighted or without authorization
- × Sharing confidential material, trade secrets, or proprietary information outside of the organization
- × Hacking into unauthorized websites
- × Sending or posting information that is defamatory to the company, its products/services, colleagues, and/or customers
- × Introducing malicious software onto the company network and/or jeopardizing the security of the organization's electronic communications systems
- × Sending or posting chain letters, solicitations, or advertisements not related to business purposes or activities
- × Passing off personal views as representing those of the organization

If an employee is unsure about what constitutes acceptable Internet usage, then he/she should ask his/her supervisor for further guidance and clarification.

All terms and conditions as stated in this document are applicable to all users of [Company name] network and Internet connection. All terms and conditions as stated in this document reflect an agreement of all parties and should be governed and interpreted in accordance with the policies and procedures mentioned above. Any user violating these policies is subject to disciplinary actions deemed appropriate by [Company name].

User compliance

I understand and will abide by this Internet Usage Policy. I further understand that should I commit any violation of this policy, my access privileges may be revoked, and disciplinary action and/or appropriate legal action may be taken.

_____   _____

Employee signature   Date

References & Bibliography

http://www.ehow.com/how_15979_hire-employees.html

http://www.informationsolutionsinc.com/blog/23-blog/56-10-steps-to-hiring-the-right-person

http://www.extension.iastate.edu/valueaddedag/info/Hiringrightand retaininggoodemployees.htm

http://www.sba.gov/content/writing-effective-job-descriptions

http://money.cnn.com/2007/05/31/magazines/fsb/hiring.managing.fsb/index.htm

http://www.communitycareers.com.au/-344683/client-newsletter-1

http://money.cnn.com/2007/05/31/magazines/fsb/hiring.managing.resources.fsb/index.htm?postversion=2007053117

http://au.smallbusiness.yahoo.com/managing/staffing/a/-/8752640/when-to-hire-a-new-employee/

http://www.macrorecruitment.com.au/index.php?category=3&section=67&article=171

http://www.entrepreneur.com/humanresources/hiring/article56398.html

http://qualityg.blogspot.com/2007/09/hiring-process-is-most-important.html

http://www.wikihow.com/Train-New-Employees

http://www.associatedcontent.com/article/230298/how_to_train_a_new_employee_so_they.html?cat=31

http://www.tarleton.edu/FINADMINWEB/hr/Performance_Management/Staff_Performance_Evaluation_Instructions.pdf

Billows, Dick. PMP. *Essentials of Project Management*. (Kindle Edition—Sep 8, 2010)—Kindle eBook

Buckingham, Marcus. *Go Put Your Strengths to Work.*
Dorio, Marc. *Boosting Employee Performance.*
Evans, G. Edward and Ward, Patricia Layzell. *Management Basics for Information Professionals, Second Edition*
Gurvis, Sandra. *Management Basics: A Practical Guide for Managers.*
Katzenbach, Jon R. *Peak Performance.*
Kreitner, Robert. Student Achievement Series: Foundations of Management: Basics and Best Practices, (Paperback—Aug 30, 2007)—Student Edition
Messmer, Harold. *Human Resources Kit for Dummies.*
Muller, Max. *The Manager's Guide to HR: Hiring, Firing, Performance Evaluations, Documentation, Benefits, and Everything Else You Need to Know*
Putzier, John and Baker, David. *The Every Thing HR KIT.*
Smart, Geoff and Street, Randy. *Who: The A Method for Hiring.*
Templar, Richard. *The Rule of Management.*
Tracy, Brian. *Full Engagement!: Inspire, Motivate, and Bring Out the Best in Your People*
—. *Hire and Keep the Best People: 21 Practical & Proven Techniques You Can Use Immediately!*

Index

CPSIA information can be obtained at www.ICGtesting.com
Printed in the USA
LVOW041018170612

286481LV00006B/44/P